DRIVEN

DRIVEN

ROSEMARY SMITH

WITH ANN INGLE

HarperCollins*Publishers*

HarperCollins*Publishers*
1 London Bridge Street
London SE1 9GF

www.harpercollins.co.uk

First published by HarperCollins*Publishers* 2018

1 3 5 7 9 10 8 6 4 2

A catalogue record of this book is
available from the British Library

ISBN 978-0-00-830185-9

All photos courtesy of the author, with the following exceptions:

Plate section: p2 (top) The Irish Newsagency Dublin; p3 (top), p10 (top right)
Independent Newspapers Ltd; p3 (bottom), p4 (top), p14 (bottom) Brian Foley; p4
(middle) Chalfont Driving Services; p5 (top) H.R. Clayton; p5 (bottom left) Graham
Vickery; p5 (bottom right) Goodchild Pictorial Photography Ltd; p6 (top and bottom)
Rootes Motors Ltd; p7 (top) Photo-Plage; p7 (bottom), p8 (top) Autosport photos/
L. Buscariet; p9 (top) Tony O'Malley; p9 (bottom left) Graphic House/Archive Photos/
Getty Images; p9 (bottom right) A. Bank Ltd; p11 (middle left) Evening Press; p11
(middle right) British Leyland; p11 (bottom) Classic Cars; p12 (top) Esler and Beatty
Crawford; p12 (bottom) Esler Crawford Photography; p13 (bottom) Continental
Photo Lab; p14 (top left) © Scott McNaughton; p14 (top right) Mark Doyle;
p16 (bottom) © Marco Mori/Renault UK

Text images: pviii Independent Newspapers Ltd; p2 Mirrorpix; p49 Bill Mansill;
p64 Daily Mail; p71 Rootes Motors Ltd; p75, p120 Waller; p87 Chrysler
Photographic; p131 Daily Mirror; p218 Eire post office

Printed and bound in Great Britain by
CPI Group (UK) Ltd, Croydon, CR0 4YY

Dedicated to Patricia (Pat) Doyle,
my lifelong friend

CONTENTS

FOREWORD BY EDDIE JORDAN   1

INTRODUCTION   5

CHAPTER 1: THE START   11

CHAPTER 2: SPECIAL STAGES   23

CHAPTER 3: 'YOU DRIVE,' SHE SAID   41

CHAPTER 4: AND WE'RE OFF!   55

CHAPTER 5: REVVING UP WITH ROOTES   61

CHAPTER 6: THE AMERICAS   81

CHAPTER 7: AVOIDABLE ACCIDENTS   95

CHAPTER 8: MOVING ON   105

CHAPTER 9: DOWN UNDER   111

CHAPTER 10: SOUTH OF THE BORDER   129

CHAPTER 11: MEN, MARRIAGE AND
    MORTGAGES   147

CHAPTER 12: RAINY KENYA   163

CHAPTER 13: RACING AROUND   173

CHAPTER 14: FROM BAD TO WORSE   181

CHAPTER 15: ROCK BOTTOM   185

CHAPTER 16: LET'S FACE IT   191

CHAPTER 17: IN BUSINESS   197

CHAPTER 18: SEEKING SOLUTIONS   201

CHAPTER 19: RECOLLECTIONS AND REGRETS 211

CHAPTER 20: DÉJÀ VU   225

CHAPTER 21: PASSION FOR LIFE   243

ACKNOWLEDGEMENTS   257
ABOUT THE AUTHORS   259
INDEX   261

FOREWORD

by Eddie Jordan

I HEAR PEOPLE these days talking non-stop about passion and commitment, and that's great, because without them there won't be success. But these two elements come after the primary vital ingredient: inspiration.

Rosemary Smith inspired a generation of young Irish drivers, myself included, to pursue our dreams of an international career. As a young lad going to Synge Street School in Dublin, I was mad about cars – inspired initially by my cousin Noel Smith, who was a fine rally driver and got his hands on a Porsche 911 from time to time. But up in the stratosphere there was a supercool Irish icon who inspired the following generation of Irish drivers that we could achieve success on the international stage – and that icon was Rosemary Smith.

Like most young car nuts of that era, I bought *Autosport* when I could, and I remember Rosemary getting the front cover for her heroic outright win in the Tulip Rally in 1965. It was the equivalent of a WRC event today. The Swinging

Sixties was in full flow in London and Paddy Hopkirk's Monte Carlo Rally wins brought the Mini (the car, not the skirt!) and motorsport on to the front pages and into the social columns. Motorsport was uber-cool and Rosemary was the queen of it. She was an Irish superstar, a Dusty Springfield lookalike who was incredibly talented behind the wheel.

In 1966 I did my Leaving Cert (A-levels) and Rosemary was entered into the RAC Rally, reports of which we followed in detail when we should have been studying.

Breakfast with Jim Clark on the RAC Rally in the 1960s

There were 150 entries headed by Jim Clark and Graham Hill – two racing world champions. The real Stig (Blomqvist) and Roger Clarke and dozens of other rally aces were joined by Rosemary in her tiny Hillman Imp. She has an incredible knack of being able to drive error-free and managed to be one of only 50 finishers, ending in a magnificent 14th place.

Rosemary was incredibly glamorous and made rallying and racing the sport we longed to be part of. She was a rare Irish driver on the world stage and it is great that in motor-sport she is still treated like royalty – in fact, better than royalty – and she deserves it.

We first met around 1975 when I was starting to race in England, with Aintree being the closest UK circuit, and she was campaigning a Ford Escort. She was a fine circuit racer who could hold her own against the best. The Renault F1 team told me in 2017 that they were going to give her a run at Paul Ricard and I was delighted.

Rosemary is a pioneer for women in motorsport and remains a great ambassador for her sport, and especially women's place in it. Hers is a remarkable story of a lifetime of success at the very highest level in one of the most male-dominated sports on the planet. It is a story every aspiring driver can draw inspiration from.

INTRODUCTION

AS I SAT behind the wheel of Renault's 800bhp Formula 1 car, my hands were sweaty, my pulse was racing and my heart was banging away in my chest. What had I let myself in for? A week before, I had been happily drinking tea and watching *Flog It* on the telly and now I was surrounded by film cameras and mechanics all yelling instructions at me. As I wedged my body into the car and the mechanics wheeled me out of the garage, I was shaking. I was nervous, terrified, but nothing was going to stop me. I hadn't felt like this since I attempted to break the Irish National Land Speed Record in 1978. As I began to drive, the noise was deafening, but all I could do was keep going as the air whistled past me. It was then that the adrenaline kicked in and I was away, without a thought for my safety or survival. The sheer excitement of it all overtook me as the engine roared and my speed increased. I had fire in my belly and I just went with it. Fright and exhilaration all at the same time, a sensation I will never forget!

It was a truly amazing experience and the only reason I became involved was because two charming men, Paddy McGee and James Boyer of Renault, suggested it. They wanted to make a documentary of the old girl driving a Formula 1 car around the Circuit Paul Ricard in France and it didn't take much to persuade me: I love a challenge. I was well known in motorsports circles in my day, having achieved notoriety for competing against, and sometimes beating, many of the male drivers, but I was never really famous until I went to Marseille in June 2017 to drive that Formula 1 racing car. After that, I received more publicity than I ever had before in my entire life. Of course, when I was driving in rallies and racing all over Europe, there was no social media to promote events and certainly no Google or YouTube. The documentary made of that Formula 1 drive has thousands of hits on YouTube and they keep telling me I have gone viral, but that just sounds like a bad dose of the flu to me!

When I was asked to go to Silverstone prior to the British Grand Prix to celebrate my Formula 1 drive, I was treated like a celebrity and that's a nice feeling when you are coming up to your 80th birthday. I've had six stents inserted, a broken collarbone, a cracked kneecap and a sprained ankle (and none of them in a car) and I survived. Eighty isn't old any longer and I see no reason to stop doing the things I love. A lot of my contemporaries are still going strong: Paddy Hopkirk, Jackie Stewart, Rauno Aaltonen – I see them all at functions and parties.

I am enjoying life to the full; running the driving school, giving private lessons and generally keeping busy. Recently, I gave a talk to a large group of people at a seminar in the International Financial Services Centre in Dublin. 'Are you sure?' I asked the woman who telephoned to ask me to do the talk, because I knew the people attending would all be highly educated with senior positions in their organisations. I only know how to drive cars and win rallies, but apparently that is enough. I rarely turn anything down, but I did a week ago when I was asked to take part in an event testing a self-driving car. 'Autonomous,' they call them. I was supposed to sit in the car with the windows blacked out and a little laptop on my knee to steer. That I declined to do!

People often ask, When are you going to retire? and I just laugh at them. Do they really believe I could sit watching television and eating marshmallows with my feet up for the rest of my life? I am glad to say that there is always something to be done. I have a huge calendar on the wall, on which I write down all my appointments, and as I sit looking at it today, my life looks very full. Last week, I had a telephone call from a man asking me to drive his car from London to Spain next year in a classic rally. I said I would, thanks very much, but these days I always include the proviso: If I'm still alive.

I contemplate death from time to time but I sorted out my funeral arrangements long ago. When my mother died, I had a headstone made for the family grave in Deansgrange and it set me thinking about how I would like to go. In 2003 I saw Adam Faith's funeral on the television and he was the first person I had ever seen buried in a wickerwork casket and I fell in love with it. I have observed so many beautiful oak coffins go through those curtains at the crematorium and I think it's a disgrace and a terrible waste of good timber! I am sure they unscrew the brass handles to be recycled before they reach the furnace, but even so …

I talked to my friend, Pat Doyle, who told me about a very good funeral parlour in Bray, County Wicklow, and I asked her to accompany me so that we could order the casket. It was a lovely place, and when we entered, a very suave gentleman approached us, looking suitably sombre. 'I want to order a coffin, please,' I said. 'It has to be a wickerwork casket and must be sprayed pink.' The man replied that this was most unusual but it could be done and then he wanted to know who had passed away. 'It's for me,' I told him. 'Could you let me know when you want it?' he asked. 'I'm not sure,' I replied, 'but my friend Pat here will let you know.'

We went out of that funeral parlour laughing our heads off and drove straight to the solicitors to make my will. I gave my solicitor details of friends and family to whom I would bequeath whatever I had left and he duly took notes. Then I told him about my visit to the funeral director and all about the pink wickerwork casket I had ordered. When I am cremated, I want the church softly lit as I look better in low lighting and nobody is to wear black, *nobody*, I told him. As my casket is wheeled up, I want the music 'Blaze Away' by Josef Locke, singing about making a bonfire of his troubles and watching them blaze away. Then, as I am going through the curtains, Andrea Bocelli and Sarah Brightman will be singing 'Time to Say Goodbye', and if you could arrange for an enormous cardboard hand to be waving at everyone that would be great. The poor solicitor is still looking at me!

The will and the funeral arrangements are all sorted but I'm not ready to say goodbye just yet, and before I go I am determined to do what so many people have suggested: tell my story. I have driven cars in rallies all over the world – Africa, Canada, Europe, Australia, New Zealand, Tasmania, you name it, I've been there – but when I started off on my career, 60 years ago, I had no idea that anybody would have the slightest interest in my story and so I didn't make notes and I have never kept a diary – when things are over, they are over as far as I'm concerned. So this is what I'm up against, but I will do my best to write about my life as honestly as my memory allows.

September 2018

CHAPTER 1

THE START

DESPITE WHAT SOME people think, I wasn't born with a silver spoon in my mouth. For some reason, people always have the impression that I come from a very wealthy family. The truth is, we were always on some sort of economy drive, although my mother did her best to ignore that. My dad, John Metcalf Smith, had a small garage in Rathmines and in the early days, when there were very few cars on the roads, there was not a great deal of business. But he was a good, kind man and people took to him and the clients he had were loyal. My dad was a Methodist and he had what I call the Protestant ethic: hard-working, reliable and straight as a die. My mother, Jane, was a Catholic, and as well as the religious divide, there was little else they had in common. As it was a mixed marriage, the ceremony took place on the side altar of the church in Dunboyne, County Meath. In the late 1920s, if a Protestant married a Catholic, a solemn promise was made whereby the children of the marriage would be brought up as Catholics. My father was scrupulous in this regard and every Sunday he dropped us all off for Mass and then went on alone to the Rathgar Methodist Church on Brighton Road.

My parents had three children in quick succession and I was the youngest of the family; Pamela was the eldest and Roger was the middle child. Pamela was beautiful, small and dark with lovely eyes. Dad's mother and father were not happy with him marrying a Catholic. Once Pamela arrived, all that changed, because she was the most adorable baby. At school, she passed every exam with flying colours but she had no interest in clothes or fashion, much to my mother's disappointment. When they went out to buy a new coat or dress, Pamela would have a book in her hand, and would barely look up when my mother asked her opinion on the item in question. Instead she just nodded her head and turned over the page. She always seemed to me to be totally self-contained; she did her own thing from a very early age. After leaving school, she went to London to study at a Montessori Teacher Training College. Pamela just wanted to get away, and who could blame her? Our home was not a peaceful one. My mother was constantly nagging and having tantrums and Dad seemed unable or reluctant to stand up to her; he adored her.

Pamela, who never smoked or drank, died of cancer when she was 64. She had five children and lived near Seattle, in the USA, in a house overlooking the Puget Sound. My mother favoured my brother, Roger. Roger was lovely and, if he were around today, he and I would be great friends. Poor Roger died tragically of a heart attack at 42 years of age, when his wife, Jackie, was pregnant with their second child. When Roger left school, he helped Dad run the garage. But the way Roger wanted to run the business was totally different from my father. Someone would come in for work to be done and Roger would give an estimate and Dad would say, 'No, no, he's a good customer and maybe he mightn't have the money.' 'Of course he's a good customer if we don't charge him,' Roger replied. I might be a millionaire now if I hadn't inherited my father's lack of business acumen.

In the early days, one of my father's customers was Jeff Smurfit, who owned a small business and rented a shed around the corner from Dad's garage in Rathmines. Sometimes his truck would break down in the middle of the night and my father thought nothing of going out to help him, whatever the time of day, much to my mother's annoyance. Mr Smurfit was always late paying his bills, which annoyed her even more. At the end of one month, the bill was particularly high and Jeff Smurfit made my father an offer: 'Instead of paying the bill, I'll give you half the business,' he said. The business was a small box company, which wasn't doing too well, and my mother didn't like this idea at all and told Dad to refuse. Sometimes you miss the boat; Dad certainly did on that occasion – Smurfit's is now a multibillion-dollar business. If only my dad had taken the chance with Mr Smurfit, if only he had let Roger run the business, if only … If 'ifs' and 'ands' were pots and pans, there'd be no work for tinkers' hands … you know that silly saying. My dad's work ethic was to do an honest day's labour without taking advantage of his customers. He lacked real business flair, however, and his heart often ruled his head, except when my mother got in the way.

Roger couldn't work with my father – their ideas on how to run a business were totally different, but they both loved cars and competed in a few races without much success, I'm sorry to say. They didn't have decent cars and despite the fact that he was a good driver, probably better than me, Roger never reached his potential. After practice he would be delighted to find himself in pole position and then in the race, after two or three laps, the car would blow up.

Roger took off to England to work for a Ford dealership and I never saw much of him after that. In their spare time, he and a friend of his drove around the countryside of Yorkshire, calling into farmhouses and cottages looking for clocks that didn't work and offering to buy them for little or nothing. 'Oh here, take it away, it hasn't worked for years,' people would say. They accumulated an assortment of clocks, which they tried to repair, not always success- fully, and then sold them on at markets and to antique shops. Roger was a very good salesman and this was a nice little sideline for a while.

My wonderful dad taught Roger, Pamela and me to swim and drive when we were very young – 'In case of emergencies,' he said. We learnt to drive in a big old-fashioned Vauxhall and I was only 11 when I first got behind the wheel. I loved it from the off; I was so small that I had to sit on cushions to see over the steering wheel. Dad had bought a field in Old Bawn, Tallaght (one of his better ideas), and we would drive round and round on the wet grass. Little did I know at the time, but this experience was to come in useful years later when I drove in the Monte Carlo rallies over those icy roads in Europe.

My dad was right about emergencies, because learning to drive at such a young age came in very handy one day. I must have been about 13 when it happened. My mother and I were alone in the kitchen in our house in Rathfarnham. She had been washing dishes in the sink and with wet hands she tried to pull the plug of the electric fire out of the socket on the wall. In those days plugs weren't earthed, and she screamed as she dropped to the stone floor, unconscious, still clutching the plug. I rushed to her side, pulled the plug from her hand and quickly decided I had to get her to a doctor. We had a telephone but for some reason it didn't occur to me to ring for my father or an ambulance – I didn't stop to think, all I was concerned with was getting help as soon as I could. I dragged my mother outside and somehow got her into the old Vauxhall parked in the driveway. The driveway was very narrow, barely the width of the car, and I bumped along, hitting the walls on either side. Somehow I managed to get out of the driveway, on to the steep hill and turn right.

I was in first gear as we chugged down to Dr Donald, who lived on our road in the first house over the bridge. He was just on his way out when we arrived and you can imagine his amazement when he saw me driving the car with my unconscious mother in the back. He gave her CPR and called an ambulance and gradually she came back to life. My mother wasn't dead and the doctor congratulated me and assured me she was going to be all right. It was then I started shaking as the enormity of what I had just done overcame me. I left the car there and ran home.

We went most years to Bettystown, a small village on the coast in County Meath, for our holidays. It was lovely there – beautiful beaches and long, lazy days of doing nothing. My father loved golf and he played in all weathers. Thunderstorms didn't bother him; he just didn't seem to care as he had a most peculiar affinity with the elements. Mother said he could have been killed with a steel club in his hand and the lightning flashing. I was preoccupied with other things and got my first kiss on the beach in Bettystown from a 14-year-old boy from Glasnevin and I thought I was in love.

On the drive to and from Bettystown, I often felt sick sitting in the back of the car. Our old car would wobble along and then, as I watched the cars flashing by out of the side window, I would get dizzy and shout to my father to stop as I was going to be sick. I only ever felt ill when someone else was driving; when I was behind the wheel, I was perfectly fine. Driving was something that I could do well and I badly needed something to boost my confidence. I was dreadfully shy, maybe because I grew so tall at a very young age, and I used to walk around with my head and shoulders down, trying to make myself smaller, my arms dangling like a gorilla.

I remember my first dance. I was sitting on a chair at the side of the hall, as was the custom: boys on one side, girls on the other. A good-looking boy crossed the floor, his dark hair stiff with Brylcreem, and asked me to dance. I was thrilled, but when I stood up I was towering over him; he made some hasty excuse and ran off. As I surveyed the boys in the hall that night, it seemed to me that they were all training to be jockeys.

It took me years to get over my shyness. It was so bad at one stage, whenever we won something in a rally, I would send my co-driver up first to collect the trophy, but once I got into a car I felt insulated and confident. I was always happiest behind the wheel. Maybe in the beginning the car was like a home for me, the only thing I had complete control over and where I felt secure. Growing up, there was little sense of security and maybe this was because our family lived in so many different locations. My mother was a nomad and never wanted to be in one residence for long. We lived in so many places: Bray, where I was born, then Dundrum, Terenure, Rathfarnham, Blackrock and Sandymount before finally settling down in Dunboyne, County Meath. I grew up falling over paint cans and ladders. When I got married I would stay in the same house all my life, I vowed, but the best-laid plans of mice and men often go awry, as the saying goes.

We lived in a beautiful house in Waltham Terrace in Blackrock for a while. It was a wreck when my parents bought it but Dad was great with his hands and with help from some friends he renovated it. There were steps up to the hall door and a basement leading out to the garden. They bought it for £8,000, and when they put it on the market a few years later it made twice as much. That was a great transaction but in most cases they would buy at the wrong time and sell again at an even worse one.

When we moved into the house at Strand Road, Sandymount, my mother loved it because the sea was on our doorstep. It had six bedrooms and she took in students from Trinity College. One evening in the kitchen of that house, with its stone-flagged floor, Mother dropped a plate and Dad mumbled something like 'That's right, drop the lot' in a jokey kind of a way. My mother took every plate she could put her hands on and smashed them to the ground deliberately, one after the other. Dad stood there looking at her, his face expressionless, without making a comment, and when everything lay shattered on the floor, he took up the brush and swept up the mess. He never reacted to anything she did, but calmly accepted it, and maybe that's where he went wrong. I believe my mother wanted him to retaliate but he never did. She got her own way all the time and that's why we moved around so much.

She could never stay in any house for long and my father just went along with her wishes.

Moving didn't really make a difference – my mother was never content, no matter where we lived, and there were constant rows, not just with my father, but all of us. She was an attractive woman and everybody who didn't have to live with her thought she was wonderful. My mother was talented, a good dressmaker, with a great sense of style, and we found out too that she could write. When Pamela went to live in America, she wrote long letters describing everything at home in such detail; she had hidden talent and so much pent-up energy. I believe she was frustrated by not having the opportunity to express herself and maybe that was why she was such a very heavy smoker. There were packets of Gold Flake and Player's around the house and my father was always begging her to give them up. Eventually, after years of smoking and a doctor's warning, she did.

Being married to my father, staying home and minding children didn't suit her, and let's face it, there were three people in their relationship: my father, my mother and my father's best friend. He was a builder and we lived for a time in a bungalow he built for them in Terenure. Poor old dad would go out the back door to go to the garage early in the morning and his best friend would come in the front door. Roger and I were told to run out into the garden and play while they talked or whatever they were doing! He was married to a woman he had met on holiday in England

and my mother was only introduced to him after she had married Dad.

Little things would upset me, like the Christmas when Dad bought my mother a beautiful Christian Dior necklace with two little diamonds; it is beautiful, I still have it. She took it from him with a very offhand thank you, but when Dad's friend came in with a handbag, pure leather, from Brown Thomas, she thanked him profusely and raved about it for weeks. She told me in later years that Dad's friend had asked her to go away with him, but she refused because of us. I often wished she had taken him up on his offer because life at home would have been happier for everyone. I used to pull my jumper over my ears so as not to hear her when she was screaming at Dad; Pamela just stuck her nose in a book and Roger would go out to get away from it all.

I once asked my father why he didn't leave her and he told me that he had tried. He went up to Belfast to join the army but his eyesight wasn't good enough and he was turned down and came back home. As he got older, his life was miserable. He suffered from Bell's palsy and had a series of mini strokes. My mother's behaviour didn't help his condition and I never really understood why she was so unkind to him.

When my brother got married in Middlesbrough, in England, we all went over for the wedding. My mother, my Aunt Lily and a family friend sat in the car during the long drive back through the Pennines, taking delight in talking about my father and his many shortcomings as if he wasn't there. I sat beside him, holding his hand, as the tears ran down his face. A trusting, loving man, he was abused by my mother and betrayed by his best friend.

My father died when he was 73 and the wife of his friend went the year after, so my mother was finally free to marry. She bought a beautiful, long, brown velvet coat and she looked absolutely gorgeous. My father's friend had two daughters and they were there in the church with their husbands on the day of the marriage. At the altar, my mother was asked by Roger, the son-in-law of the man she was about to marry, to sign a pre-nuptial agreement waiving all rights to his fortune. She did as she was asked without any fuss or question. It amazed me that the family could possibly have thought she was after his money; surely they must have known that this affair had been going on for over 40 years?

I loved my father and we had a great relationship – he was always my biggest supporter. He was a wonderful husband; he never looked at another woman, never drank alcohol or smoked. Everything was for my mother, but she didn't appreciate any of that and made life a misery with her constant yelling, slamming doors and generally behaving like a spoilt child. Her animosity towards my father seemed to spill over on to me. Nothing I ever did was quite right in her eyes, from how I did my hair to choosing a husband. Mother–daughter relationships are often troubled, but ours was particularly so. She did nothing to help my confidence; it was Dad who did his best to encourage me, yet she knew I had talent. But my mother endeavoured to fulfil some of her own ambitions and aspirations through me, especially after I left school.

CHAPTER 2

SPECIAL STAGES

I WENT TO Beaufort High School in Rathfarnham, run by the Loreto nuns. The nuns wore hard white wimples covering their foreheads so not a wisp of hair could be seen, a black veil over the top, a long black habit, and they smelt of carbolic soap. Our uniform was no better. We were made to wear a chocolate brown pinafore dress, with a square neck with pleats at the front, which made the girls who had a bit of a bosom look huge, and the sash belts tied around our middles didn't help. A yellow and brown striped tie, a beige jumper and brown knickers with elastic around our knees completed the hideous outfit. I hated every bit of it and I've never worn brown since.

I was popular with some of my classmates because I was always ready for a bit of devilment. I loved playing hockey but the nun in charge always put me in goal because she didn't like me. She would referee running around the pitch with her habit tucked into the cord at her waist. One rainy morning when we were playing, she ran towards the goal, calling out to the girls to shoot. I put out my hockey stick and deliberately tripped her up. Sister went down with a bang, and when she got up she was covered in mud from head to foot. My friends loved that because she was a particularly nasty woman, whom we all detested. I had a lot of friends at school, some of whom I still see. Doris Joyce was one of the best and the last person in the world you would think would become a nun. My cousin Noelle was in my class and very kindly says today that she doesn't remember what a disastrous student I was.

I disliked most everything about school but I developed other passions to make up for it. I loved driving and I adored my riding classes at Iris Kellett's school in Mespil Road. It was seven shillings and sixpence a lesson and it was a good thing that Pamela and Roger weren't interested, as my father complained about the cost and certainly wouldn't have stretched the budget to allow all three of us to attend. Iris Kellett was the only child of a veterinary surgeon who had left the British Army to help start up Kellett's, a drapery business in Georges Street. He also acquired the British Army cavalry stables in Mespil Road and Iris helped him run it as a riding school. Iris was a brilliant equestrian and during her lifetime she became known and respected internationally.

Iris took us down to Sandymount Strand very early in the morning and I had a little pony, Penny, who was very docile and sweet until she got on the beach and then she ran and ran, leaving me hanging on for dear life. I competed in gymkhanas and eventually in the RDS in Ballsbridge, when I rode a pony called Lauralie. This was a great achievement for me and I was thrilled with myself. I cantered around and then, when I got to the first jump, Lauralie stopped dead. You are allowed two refusals, and next time she approached the fence she was over it in a flash. We cantered around, taking all the jumps after that, and were doing well until the fence at the top of the arena when the pony stopped dead, and this time I went flying over. The pony looked at me and seemed to laugh as I picked myself up to do the walk of shame back down past the big stand, where all the children were sniggering at my downfall.

I was more successful playing golf with my father in Rathfarnham. I was good at it, but hated all the rules and regulations, and the clothes that some of the women wore were horrendous. I had a handicap of 12 when I had to give it up because of a problem with my back and I have never played since.

I loved tennis and joined the Sandyford Tennis Club and soon became a team member. Going away to compete against other clubs was great fun. Anything to do with physical activity makes me happy but don't ask me to sit still and concentrate. I'll never understand how my sister and brother found studying so easy.

At school, there were no ponies, no golf, no cars or tennis, nothing that interested me. I was good at sport, sewing, geography and art, but that was about all. I really didn't apply myself or care for that matter and I believe it might have been the Irish exam that brought the wrath of the head nun down on my head. I put my name at the top of the page, Rósmáire Ní Gowan, and then proceeded to draw lots of little horses jumping over fences. At the end of the exam, I just folded my paper and handed it in. I got 1 per cent – I think that must have been for writing my name in Irish!

The Mother Superior rang my father and asked him to come in to discuss my progress. When they met, the nun didn't hold back. 'Mr Smith,' she said, 'your daughter is stupid.' To this day, I believe what Mother Superior meant was I had the brains but I was stupid because I wouldn't use them; that's what I like to think anyway. My father didn't take it like that and he was furious. 'No nun is going to tell me that my daughter is stupid,' he said, his prejudice coming to the fore, and he removed me from the school straight away, even though I was only 15. I can't remember being particularly upset by this decision and I spent a very happy summer, left to my own devices.

My mother wasn't pleased at the prospect of having me hanging around the house. Roger was helping my father run the business, Pamela was studying in London, and so Mother made the decision to send me to the Grafton Academy of Fashion Design. She had taught me to sew and knew that I was good with a needle and thread. I always loved clothes and as a child made dresses for my dolls, which were much admired by my friends and relatives. I had one particular favourite doll that had a papier mâché head; the rest of her body was stuffed. Unfortunately, I left her outside one night and it spilled rain and the whole doll's body and face were ruined, not to mention her taffeta dress. I was heartbroken.

The Grafton Academy was Ireland's first fashion design school and was at the heart of the Irish fashion industry. It was run by a pioneering woman, Mrs Pauline Clotworthy, who opened the Academy in 1938. She had been trained at the British Institute of Dress Designing alongside Hardy Amies and Norman Hartnell, who was later to become Queen Elizabeth's couturier. Pauline Clotworthy was determined to pass on her knowledge and expertise to young people in Ireland. Over the years, the Academy has trained many of the country's leading designers and I hoped I could be one of them.

Sending me to the Academy was one of my mother's better ideas and I started there in September 1953, a month after my 16th birthday. Mrs Clotworthy was a wonderful teacher with endless patience and she took a great interest in me and my work. I was happy there because I was well able to follow instruction outside of the dreaded school environment. I found the art of dressmaking came easily and all the teachers were very encouraging and complimentary about my efforts. I was meant to be undertaking a two-year course but in the following April, after only eight months, I asked if I could graduate with the students who had been studying for two years. At first Mrs Clotworthy said it couldn't be done but when she saw some of my work she relented.

In order to graduate I had to make four outfits, which I modelled myself. When I wore the beachwear I'm sure I looked like a scarecrow. I was 5'10", which I still am today, and a size 8, which I am no longer. I made the evening dress out of felt and no one had ever used that fabric before in dresses. I will never forget that bright pink, strapless dress; the front was knee-length and the back went right to the ground and I stuck big black felt circles around the end of the skirt and even had shoes dyed to match. On the day of the graduation I nearly collapsed when the results were announced: Rosemary Smith, Overall Student of the Year.

From the Academy, I went to the boutique of Irene Gilbert in South Frederick Street, Dublin, the street famed for fashion houses at the time. Irene Gilbert was a very shy woman but that didn't stop her from being the first woman to run a successful fashion business in Ireland and becoming a famous couturier. She used tweed material to great effect and liaised with the mills to create the exact colours she wanted.

Some people preferred Sybil Connolly, another great Irish designer, because of her fabrics, especially the pleated linen, for which she was famous, but to my mind no one could touch Irene Gilbert. One of her most famous creations was a Carrickmacross lace evening dress commissioned by Princess Grace, and she also dressed many celebrities in Ireland, including Phyllis Ryan, the wife of

President Seán T. O'Kelly. I was privileged to be working with her as an apprentice and she taught me a great deal. She had the most wonderful finish on her garments and taught me all linings must be hand sewn, hooks and eyes must not be seen. Now I was on my way to becoming a dress designer and, for many years, the press always hung that qualification on to the end of everything – Rosemary Smith, Dress Designer, wins whatever. What the dress designing had to do with the driving was beyond me but maybe it drew attention to the fact that I was a woman in a man's world.

There was no real chance to show off my dress designing skills working for Irene Gilbert, as my position in her studio was such a modest one. I was ambitious and left to try my luck at designing for T. J. Cullen, a company situated along the quays, where Temple Bar is now. Old Mrs Cullen was a formidable woman who moved with the aid of a walking stick and managed the place with great authority. My wages were two pounds, eight shillings and eight pence per week and as we lived in Sandyford at the time I had to get up at seven in the morning to catch the 44 bus to work.

I designed two summer dresses, which the buyers liked, and Cullen's got orders to make 100 dozen of each garment. I asked Mrs Cullen for a rise on the strength of that and she gave me another halfpenny an hour! Una Tapley was in charge of cutting out the fabric and when she started the machine one day, a rat suddenly ran across the factory floor. Una lost concentration and the saw cut off the top of her finger. Blood was spurting everywhere, all over the material, and everybody was screaming.

Mrs Cullen came out of the office and asked what all the fuss was about. 'Una's cut the top of her finger off,' I told her. 'Very careless,' Mrs Cullen said. 'She has destroyed all this material.' Mrs Cullen stopped the cost of the fabric from Una's wages, but nobody was surprised – that was how things were in those days. Una went to the hospital that day and she never came back. After that, I couldn't bear working there any more.

I was restless and I suppose my family wanted me to make use of my talents, such as they were. It was my Uncle Jimmy, who was walking behind me one day, who suggested it. He poked me in the back with his walking stick as I slouched along. 'Be proud of your height,' he said to me. 'Stand up straight, Rosemary.' Even to this day, I have to remember to make a conscious effort to stand tall. My mother agreed with him about my posture and that's how it was that she enrolled me with the Miriam Woodbyrne Modelling Agency in South Frederick Street to learn deportment. I was taught how to glide rather than walk, swivel my head, pose for photographers and make best use of my long legs, skinny body and blonde hair.

Miriam was a lovely lady, very motherly and caring, and gave me great encouragement. It was a case of being in the right place at the right time because Christian Dior brought a collection to Brown Thomas in Dublin called the New

Look. The dresses had billowing skirts, tiny wasp waists and soft rounded shoulders. Adrienne Ring, another model, and I were the only Irish girls at the agency with the right figure for his clothes. Adrienne was beautiful. She was dark, I was blonde, so we looked well together, and Dior brought some of his own models from Paris as well. I loved modelling but didn't realise at the time that this experience would be so beneficial to my career in the motor industry. At 18 years of age I thought that fashion was going to be my life. I had no idea that one day I would be sitting on top of the bonnet of a car, flashing my legs for the photographers.

My mother was a very good dressmaker and she suggested that we open a little boutique together. It wasn't like the boutique dress shops you see today – we didn't sell dresses off the peg, but designed and made dresses to order. I was in good company as Ib Jorgensen was also designing dresses in a similar set-up in Dublin.

Our shop was upstairs at 23 South Anne Street in Dublin and had a back room, which we furnished with a lovely antique desk and big ornate standing mirrors, where clients came for fittings. The front room was where we did the cutting and sewing for the bespoke garments. Dad's best friend financed the setting up of the business and on the first day we opened he took us for a celebratory meal in the Royal Hibernian Hotel, then one of the most fashionable places to eat in Dublin. I ate unfamiliar food and drank champagne for the first time that day; that night, I was very sick and vowed never to drink again!

We employed a wonderful machinist, as well as Betty, who came to work for us as a finisher and a go-for to assist us. Betty was about my age, we were both young and innocent and mad keen on pop music. We loved The Beatles but I am a little embarrassed to say that the only singer that ever really got to me was Adam Faith, a British teen idol from London, who was in the charts non-stop. He had developed this sexy way of singing, pronouncing every word in a distinctive way, which sent me, and thousands of other girls, crazy. When he came to Dublin, Betty and I went to the Theatre Royal to see him. There were the usual supporting acts but I can't remember any of them; I was impatient to see Adam, everyone else was irrelevant. When he finally appeared on stage the audience erupted and sang along to his latest hit: 'What Do You Want If You Don't Want Money?' Betty and I knew what we wanted!

We found out that he was going to appear at the Pavilion Ballroom in Blackrock, County Louth, and that was when Betty and I became groupies. I drove us to Blackrock in great excitement. When Adam came on the stage and I saw him up close, just a few feet away, he was even more adorable; he was gorgeous, tiny but gorgeous. Betty and I stood close to the stage and somehow he noticed me – well, I suppose at 5'10", with long legs, blonde hair, painted-on freckles and screaming into his face, he could hardly miss me. As he was leaving the stage, he came over, stood beside me and asked my name. I looked down at him – he was only up to my shoulder – and I stammered: 'Rosie.'

We went backstage afterwards and Adam and I got on very well. Mind you, he did most of the talking, because I was breathless and, in any case, had nothing to say. We just sort of clicked, as they say. I know now that Adam was a notorious womaniser but at the time I imagined he only had eyes for me. He said how much he loved Irish girls and their red hair, which upset me a bit, and I decided there and then that I would become a redhead. He went back to England and he telephoned from time to time and sent me postcards.

Adam was playing Dick Whittington in the Wimbledon Theatre later that year and asked would I like to come to the pantomime to see him. Would I what? I was surprised that my mother made no objection and she said I could stay with my sister Pamela, who was by then married and living in London. So I dyed my hair and discovered, much to my annoyance, that you need a special complexion for bright red hair, which I didn't have, but the damage was done. I made a skin-tight green dress to get the real Irish look and made sure to wear dead flat shoes. At the time I thought I was the bee's knees, but looking back I'm not so sure.

The tickets were there at the box office with a little note saying that I should come backstage after the show and we could go for something to eat. The theatre was magnificent, all brown and rose-pink with hints of cream and gold, a bit like the Theatre Royal in Dublin. As I looked around me I thought I was in heaven, and when I sat in my seat in the stalls and he blew me a kiss, I was ready to pass out.

When I went backstage, he introduced me to Eve Taylor, his manager, and we were supposed to go out to dinner but he was too tired. He was living with Eve and her husband at the time and it was taken for granted that I would stay with them. When we got back to the house, we had a drink and then Adam said he was going to bed, which was under-standable, considering he had spent most of the evening onstage with a cat, trying to become the Lord Mayor of London.

We went upstairs and he brought me into the bedroom and I realised then that we were meant to be sleeping together in the same bed. He got undressed and got into the bed and was fast asleep in no time. I took off my shoes and maybe I might have undressed but I had on one of those waspie things – waist clinchers, they were called – and I didn't want him to see me in that. I climbed on to the bed, and as I lay there it dawned on me that, although he was asleep now, eventually he was going to wake up. I wasn't ready for what might happen when he did. I waited, think-ing what to do, and then made my decision: I crept down-stairs, opened the hall door, never thinking there would be an alarm, and left the house behind me with the bells ring-ing in my ears. I didn't care, I was out of there.

I met Adam in London 30 years later. He had been in a TV series, *Budgie*, which was now a musical, playing at the Cambridge Theatre in the West End of London. A friend of mine told me she had heard that he had afternoon tea every day in Harvey Nichols and suggested we go along. He remembered me, or at least he said he did, but the magic was gone: we were both that much older and wiser.

The boutique in South Anne Street continued to attract custom, although I felt we could do better. When we received an order from Cutex, the nail polish company, who were bringing out a new shade of pink, I was delighted. They had heard about us and asked me to make a dress in exactly the same colour as the polish. This was just the kind of publicity we needed, and the business flourished after that.

In celebration of the success of the company, for my 21st birthday present my father decided to drive us to Spain. It was my first time on the continent and I was very excited – I didn't realise at the time that driving the roads of Europe would be something I was to become very familiar with. We stayed in Sitges, a historic town on the Mediterranean coast, where the beaches were wonderful. It was so different from Ireland and I loved it.

The following year, my good friend, Mairéad Whelan, and I decided to go on our own. I met Mairéad through rugby. Her father, who was President of the Old Belvedere Rugby Club, got us tickets for the matches in Lansdowne Road. We sat in the front row, sometimes holding our see-through plastic umbrellas, enthusiastically watching the players running around in their short shorts and blowing them kisses. I don't think they ever noticed us.

It was no easy trip because, first, there was the ferry to Liverpool, then a train to London, another to Dover and the journey across the English Channel to France and yet another train. Two young women travelling alone in Franco's Spain attracted attention and we met some amazing people along the way. We were late arriving in Barcelona that first night and missed the train to Sitges. Exhausted, and not sure where we were going to sleep, we sat drinking coffee in an almost deserted bar. Our salvation came in the form of two tall American men in naval uniform with fancy epaulettes and medals on their chests. It turned out they were officers on a huge naval vessel moored in Barcelona and offered us accommodation in the stateroom of the ship. We looked at one another, wondering if this was a wise move, but we went with them anyway. They were intrigued that two Irish women were travelling alone and seemed genuine in their concern for us. We needn't have worried as they behaved like perfect gentlemen and the stateroom they gave us to sleep in was fit for royalty.

One of the officers appeared to be well connected and spoke in familiar terms about the Kennedys. He told us that Jackie Kennedy had been offered one million dollars to stay with John F. Kennedy until after the presidential election in 1960. He obviously didn't think much of Jackie as he said she was an odd woman.

The next morning they gave us breakfast and brought us back to the station and we got the train to Sitges. We stayed in Sitges, in a little old house in the centre of the town, for three weeks and had a ball. We lazed about on the beach, swam in the sea and in the evening we watched the Flamenco dancers and enjoyed the nightlife.

It was beside a pool on that holiday that I followed my father's swimming instructions in an attempt to save a little girl's life. As I lay on my sunbed beside the pool, I heard a splash and a scream and saw a young child disappearing under the water. I dived into the pool without a thought and grabbed the child by her long blonde hair and dragged her over to the side of the pool, only to be berated by several members of her family, who shouted at me in Spanish. Apparently the child was not as young as I thought; she was a good little swimmer and had only been playing. I never practised my life-saving skills again.

The trips abroad were wonderful but I still had to concentrate on making sure the business was successful and that meant hard work and long hours. Everything was going fine until I made a big mistake. I designed and sewed the clothes for a wedding: the bride's wedding dress, six bridesmaids' dresses, the mother of the bride's dress, the bride's going away outfit, everything. We worked on those dresses for three months and borrowed to pay for the fabric, which was the very best quality. The young lady in question married a very wealthy man and, although I pursued both of them, I never got paid. I still have the wedding photographs as a constant reminder of my lack of business sense, or maybe it's just my trusting nature.

I dreamed up other ways of making money but unfortunately, for one reason or another, they didn't work. TLC was the name of one product I invented, which stood for Trouser Lining Company and also, of course, tender loving care. In the 1950s tailored trousers were becoming popular and the more expensive ones were lined. I thought that it would be brilliant to be able to buy lining as a separate item so that they could be worn underneath any pair of slacks. I made samples in white, black and cream, and Roches Stores was very interested. I tried to get them made in Ireland, but the cost was prohibitive so I researched having them made in China, but the company there wanted to know how many thousands of pairs I would be wanting, so that idea went out of the window.

I struggled on for a while but my heart wasn't in it. Fortunately, a new friendship offered a welcome distraction. Delphine Bigger was one of our customers who came in for shirts and trousers to be made, which was quite unusual at the time. She ran the Coffee Inn in South Anne Street and was married to Frank Bigger, who, together with Ronnie Adams and Derek Johnston, won the Monte Carlo Rally in 1956. At enormous expense, Delphine bought Hermès scarves from Brown Thomas, and I would transform them into blouses. They were £29 each, which was an enormous amount then, and three were needed for each blouse. I thought her the most exotic and extraordinary person I had ever met, and although we were worlds apart we got on very well.

I was at a bit of a loose end when one day Delphine asked me to go on a rally with her. I agreed without knowing just what I was letting myself in for. She didn't tell me that I was going to navigate until we arrived in Kilkenny, but I would have gone anyway. Looking back now, I must have had a sense that this was to be a significant turning point in my life, and so it was.

CHAPTER 3

'YOU DRIVE,' SHE SAID

DELPHINE WAS 10 years older than me; a striking woman with a head of thick wiry hair and an imposing stature, one of those larger-than-life characters you sometimes meet. She was a woman of the world and, among other things, she taught me to drink. She introduced me to gin and orange, which I didn't take to, too sticky and sickly for my liking, so I replaced it with vodka and tonic, but I never really got into the habit until much later.

Delphine was fond of a good time and used rallying as an excuse to get away from her husband and flirt with other men. But it took me a while to work that out, naïve and innocent as I was. It was convenient for her to have a woman with her and that's why she asked me to go along when she went rallying. 'We're going to Kilkenny on Sunday,' she said, 'and you are going to navigate.' She knew I could drive but hadn't thought to ask whether I could read a map, which I can't, even to this day. We got in the car and she handed me a map and a list of reference numbers. I kept turning the map as we went around corners and telling her to turn left and right. After about three miles we found ourselves in somebody's farmyard. My dad never cursed and Mum might say 'damn' now and again, so when Delphine began to swear at me that day I truly didn't understand what she was saying. The words she shouted were all new to me, she might as well have been speaking Swahili, but I could tell she was cross!

'I hope you drive better than you navigate. Get in the bloody car!' she snapped, getting out and leaving the door open for me to get in the driver's seat. In between giving me instructions, she was muttering and cursing, and so I did what I was told until eventually we got back on the road. As we neared the finish, Delphine told me to get out of the car. 'It wouldn't do for you to be seen driving,' she said, so we changed places.

This business of changing places went on for weeks and nobody knew that I was doing the driving until one day we were found out. In front of us that day there was a car upside down in a ditch. I slowed down and Delphine was adamant that we shouldn't stop, but for once I took no notice. I pulled over and asked, could we do anything, but the man sitting on the side of the road with a broken arm said that someone else had already gone for help. To tell the truth, if I had been more experienced I probably wouldn't have stopped to enquire how the man in the ditch was; sentiment has no place in rallying. When we arrived at the finish, word had got around that I was seen in the driver's seat and Delphine wasn't happy, but she decided that as people knew anyway it would make sense for me to drive permanently.

When I eventually realised that Delphine had a boyfriend on the side and that I was only being brought along as a sort of decoy, I didn't complain. I was having great fun and loved every minute of our monthly events, but that Circuit of Leinster rally when the accident happened nearly ruined everything. We started in the evening and we were driving through the night; it was three o'clock in the morning and in my experience that is the time when the body is at its lowest ebb, both mentally and physically. Delphine was navigating and as we were coming to a crossroad she told me to go straight ahead. It was foggy, the road was wet and slippery as I followed her instructions, only to find she had directed me to a T end, not a crossroad, and there was a resounding crash as we ran straight into a stone wall.

We were in a Mini and in those days the sun visor was held on with a metal clip. The impact of the crash caused Delphine to fall forward and the front of her head hit the metal of the visor and was sliced open. Blood was streaming down her face and she was unconscious, just slumped there and not responding. I had a torch, a scarf and a box of tissues in the car, and instinctively I knew what I had to do. I pulled the flap of skin back in place on her forehead, grabbed a bunch of tissues, put them on the top of her head and wrapped the scarf around the whole lot as tightly as I could.

I was frantic to get help, but when I tried to get out of the car the door was jammed tight. The windows in the Mini then were made of Perspex, but I managed to force my way out and set off down the road in the freezing fog, torch in hand. As always in situations like this, my shoes were left behind, so there I was, covered in blood, stumbling down a country road in the middle of the night, barefoot. Away in the distance I saw a light in a farmhouse, and as I approached dogs started to bark. I banged on the door and a man opened an upstairs window with a shotgun in his hands as he looked down at me.

'I think I've killed my co-driver. I need help,' I shouted up at him.

'Women shouldn't be driving anyway,' was his muttered reply.

He came down, and when he saw the state I was in he went back into the house for his keys. He didn't have a car, just a cattle truck. He had been to the mart that morning so the truck was stinking to high heaven and full of cow dung.

We drove back to the car and the farmer banged away at the buckled door with a sledgehammer. We managed to pull the unconscious Delphine out and carried her into the smelly truck. She groaned as we moved her and I was so glad to hear that moan because it meant she was still alive. The farmer drove us to a hospital in Goresbridge, County Carlow, which I remember thinking at the time was a very appropriate name, considering Delphine and I were covered in blood.

When we arrived at the hospital the nurse informed us that all the doctors were at a party and we would have to go to Carlow, 14 miles away. She telephoned to the hospital, telling them to expect us, and there was a doctor and nurse waiting when we arrived. They put poor Delphine on a stretcher so short that her head was hanging over the end; she had lost so much blood, the doctor didn't think she would live. She was wheeled away to an operating theatre, and as I sat there in a daze a doctor came over to attend to my face. I hadn't realised it but there was a gash on my cheek and the doctor decided I needed stitches. I think he might have been one of the doctors who had been at that party the nurse had told us about, because the smell of alcohol as he leant over me was potent, although it might have been ether. He began work on my face but he didn't use any injection or anaesthetic, just sewed me up with what looked like a large carpet needle. It didn't matter; I was beyond feeling anything anyway.

I lay on the bed in the Accident and Emergency and must have dozed for a while and then woke to find that Delphine was out of surgery. She had 49 stitches across her hairline but she was alive and that was all I cared about. I telephoned Delphine's husband, Frank, with the bad news. I told him the Mini was a write-off, but Delphine was fine. He didn't seem to care about the car and said he would come and get me straight away.

Frank arrived in a lovely little Triumph Herald to take me home. When we left the hospital I went to get into the passenger seat and he said, 'Where do you think you're going?' He insisted that I got into the car and drove home from Carlow to Dunboyne in County Meath to my house. It took us four hours and I was shaking from exhaustion and delayed shock. He kept putting his hand on the steering wheel to keep us on the road. Frank knew that if he didn't make me drive I might never get behind the wheel again.

When we arrived home I was in a terrible state. I had a black eye, there was blood all over my clothes, mostly Delphine's, and my face was swollen from the stitches. Dad was very calm and told me to have a bath and go straight to bed. The next day after breakfast he said that we were going to Laytown. Once again I went to get in the passenger seat but my father insisted I should drive. He did exactly the same thing as Frank, and to my amazement we were only a mile from the house when I was driving normally without any bother. Any of the accidents I had after that, and thank goodness I didn't have too many, I did what my father and Frank had told me to do: I just carried on.

Delphine recovered well and after a few weeks she was home and raring to go. She was lucky that she had a very low hairline and with that wonderful hair cascading around her face the scar never showed. Delphine never held the accident against me – she knew she was the one who was navigating and I was just obeying orders – but nevertheless I was relieved that we were still the best of friends. She didn't let a little thing like a crash into a wall affect her, and with a new boyfriend in tow we were back on the road to do weekend rallies and test drives.

Frank Bigger pushed me to enter rallies with Delphine; he had a high opinion of my driving abilities and also the money to back us. After a number of two-day rallies, we went for the big event: the Circuit of Ireland in 1959. In its heyday, just about everyone with an interest in motorsport migrated to Killarney, County Kerry, at Easter. People came from all over Ireland just to be part of it. Killarney was buzzing and it was nearly impossible to get somewhere to stay.

The Circuit of Ireland differed from many other rallies as it was run over closed roads. The organisers tried to keep the route secret but this was frustrated by the fact that six months before the event advertisements had to be placed in local and national newspapers to let people know that roads in their area would be closed. Three weeks prior to the rally the organisers arrived to tell local residents when and for how long the road would be out of bounds. This didn't go down too well with some of the clergy as the rally took place at Easter and they were anxious that the parishioners would be able to fulfil their religious duties.

In 1965 a farmer and his wife blocked the road near Croom in County Limerick. When a car halted, the farmer banged the windscreen with a stick and his wife threw a stone at the rear window as the drivers drove away, bypassing the blockade. But that was an exception; generally people were enthusiastic and lined the route all around the country, cheering us on.

The other significant factor in the Circuit of Ireland Rally was that pace notes were banned. In rallying, pace notes are used to describe the route to be driven, the speed anticipated to complete each stage and the turnings and junctions. Without pace notes, what you rely on is instinct, a good car, a good crew and the sheer joy of competing – and if you're lucky, winning. Nowadays rallies use notes supplied by the organisers, or alternatively, competitors are allowed to make a full reconnaissance as opposed to rallying the stages blindly. Although pace notes were banned, that didn't prevent some people from cheating and it was very difficult to get around that despite the best efforts of the marshals.

The Circuit is still held today but it is not the same as it is restricted to a short route, mostly in the north of Ireland. In the early days the Circuit was a 1,200- to 1,500-mile event (depending on the chosen route) that encompassed the whole island of Ireland. It became an important event on the rallying calendar, with drivers coming from the United Kingdom and further afield to compete.

The rally went on day and night and was hard going, but I loved it. Cars would leave Belfast on Friday night, although some years they allowed drivers to start from different locations, just like the Monte Carlo rallies, and we were able to set off from Dawson Street in Dublin one year. Typically, the route took us over the Mourne Mountains through Friday night and then down the east coast to finish in Killarney on Saturday evening. On Sunday we drove around the Ring of Kerry, then right up the west coast to Donegal on Monday. On Tuesday we drove east across Northern Ireland to finish in Bangor for the prize-giving.

As I have said, the Circuit of Ireland was always run over the Easter weekend, and sometimes there would be snow in the southwest on the Tim Healy Pass. I drove a little Hillman Imp for many of the Circuit of Ireland events and it was perfect for the narrow and twisty road around the lakes and over the mountains. I have driven in the Circuit of Ireland Rally at least eight times, winning the Ladies' Award on numerous occasions, and was placed high over-all many times. In 1968 I was third overall when Roger

My faithful Imp

Clark came first in a Ford Escort, Adrian Boyd second in a Mini Cooper and I drove my faithful Imp.

I brought that Imp, EDU 710C, back to Ireland in 2003, after it had been discovered, dismantled in a hay barn on a Hampshire farm, by Imp specialist Clark Dawson. The farmer also kept horses, and pinned to a wall of the barn behind all the horseshow rosettes was the tax disc. Clark telephoned the car registration office in Swansea and they confirmed that the number had not been transferred to another vehicle. He spent two years meticulously restoring that little car and wouldn't let me pay him for his expertise and hard work – he just told me to take my Imp home and drive it.

Thanks to my good friends John and Cepta Sheppard, my Imp has been kept in pristine condition ever since. John started the Imp Club of Ireland and I am very proud to say he made me honorary president. That Imp has appeared in *Classic Car* magazines and I have driven it in many events in Ireland and the UK ever since.

The Circuit of Ireland rallies were great, but Delphine became more ambitious and decided we would enter the RAC Rally in Britain. This was madness as we were totally unprepared and inexperienced, but she was determined and of course I was happy to go along with it and do as I was told.

That first RAC Rally in November 1961 with Delphine was a great learning experience and stood to me when I drove in the rally again in 1965 with Susan Reeves and then in 1966 with Valerie Domleo. The RAC Rally at that time meant driving for 2,400 miles over five days and three nights, with only one proper overnight stop. Today's rallies cannot compare to this, but we thought nothing of it then.

Unlike the Circuit of Ireland, the closure of public roads in Britain was impossible due to traffic restrictions. In 1960 the organisers of the RAC Rally persuaded the Forestry Commission to open up some of its closed roads for competitors, so they could drive flat out, away from the traffic regulations of the public roads. They opened up 200 miles of forest roads. The roads through the forest were mud and grit and the only other vehicles that ever went through were trucks. This meant the track had a grass mound in the middle with two big dips either side. We bumped along the uneven road and if anybody came up behind, wanting to pass, we had to pull over as quickly as possible, otherwise we would get pushed out of the way. That was the way it was because each of the stages was timed so speed was all-important.

Driving in the dark was especially difficult on those forest roads. Our little Mini had a spotlight on the roof and Delphine put her hand up to swivel the handle of the lamp whenever she saw we were coming to a bend.

Typically, the start and finish points of the RAC Rally were at the Excelsior Hotel, near Heathrow Airport, outside London. The rally started on Saturday morning and the route went west to Dorset and Somerset, then north through Wales for the night drive, where we encountered mountain tracks and treacherous surfaces, which were a nightmare. Once through Wales, we drove on through the Lake District and into Scotland, with a breakfast stop Monday morning at Bathgate. The only overnight stop was at Aviemore in the Scottish Highlands. Tuesday morning, we set off to go south via Dumfries and into the Yorkshire forests. We managed to finish that RAC Rally, and, considering it was our first time, we didn't do too badly.

Delphine, by this time, had moved into a flat on Sussex Road in Dublin 4. They were called 'flats' then but no one seems to use that word in Ireland these days, not even for the tiniest of properties. I think we must have adopted the word from America over the years, like so many other things. Mespil Flats were one of the first purpose-built apartment blocks in Dublin, and they were magnificent. Delphine's flat was pure luxury, with high ceilings, timber floors, central heating and two spacious bedrooms. In the basement there was a laundry with tumble-dryers and on the roof was a beautiful garden and, of course, a lift. The height of sophistication was the intercom system so she could let people in without having to leave the flat, just like in the movies. I had never seen anything like it before and loved going there to visit and often stayed overnight.

When the drivers came over from Britain to race at the Phoenix Park and Dunboyne races, Delphine would hold great parties in the flat, to which everyone was invited and the shenanigans were mighty. I had started racing in the Phoenix Park and I received quite a lot of attention from the male drivers but wasn't quite sure what to do with it. It was good for my ego, but I was reluctant to get involved. At 23 years of age, and still a virgin, I was on the lookout for someone special, I suppose, and as it turned out it wasn't one of those racing men I fell for.

I drove out to Bray one evening to meet some friends. As I sat waiting in the hotel lounge, a man at the bar looked over and raised his glass. 'Can I join you?' he called. Could he what! He was tall, handsome, with wonderful deep brown, 'come to bed' eyes and a voice that sounded like British aristocracy. We chatted and he told me he was filming in Ardmore Studios and had spent the day swashbuckling his way around the Wicklow countryside. He was playing Lord Melton in *Sword of Sherwood Forest* alongside Richard Greene and Peter Cushing, and his name was Oliver Reed.

We spent nearly every evening of his three-month stay in Ireland together. It was a brief but unforgettable experience and a welcome interlude before the next big rally. I drove out to Bray every evening in a flurry of excitement, to hear how filming had gone that day. Oliver was fascinating and interested in me, which I found unbelievable and very flattering. He was different from any man I had ever met, and I thought I was in love. I didn't know at the time that he was married to an Irish girl, Kate Byrne, or that she was pregnant. But my conscience is clear because although we had a great time together he was not unfaithful to his wife with me in any physical way – I wasn't ready for that!

When Oliver left to return to England, he was not entirely truthful with me. He didn't tell me about his wife but said that he was being forced to marry a daughter of one of the film producers in order to further his career. I commiserated with him about the unfairness of it all. He was some storyteller, but what a charmer!

It was about eight or nine years later when I met him again. I was with a crowd of male drivers at the airport, waiting to fly out to rally somewhere, when they all started whispering and nudging one another: 'Look who it is!' Oliver Reed, in the years since I had last seen him, had become famous, especially after playing Bill Sykes in the film *Oliver!* He had also gained a reputation as a hard drinker and was continuously in the newspapers for some escapade or other. When he saw me, he came straight over and put his arms around me and we chatted until his flight was called. He didn't look quite as handsome as I remembered him but that didn't matter. As I stood beside him all the memories came flooding back. Everyone looked at us as we reminisced about our time together in Bray. My colleagues saw me with new eyes and my reputation soared after that. They thought I was just the dumb blonde there to make the cars look good, but being a friend of Oliver Reed, that made them think again.

After our success in the rallies together, Delphine was all set with plans for more outings for the two of us but they didn't happen because in early December 1961 I received a telegram that was to change everything.

CHAPTER 4

AND WE'RE OFF!

OUT OF THE blue, in December 1961, Sally Anne Cooper sent me a telegram asking me to drive with her in a Sunbeam Rapier for the Monte Carlo Rally the following January. I had never heard her name before and had no idea who she was, or why she had picked me, but I was delighted with the idea. I could only guess that someone must have seen me driving in the RAC Rally and told her about me, but I was never sure if that was true or who it might have been. My father said that the Coopers were a famous family, who had made their fortune from insect repellent aerosols in England.

After that telegram, I spoke with Sally Anne by telephone and she told me she was getting married in May. She wanted to do something glamorous and exciting before she began her married life and had decided that the Monte Carlo Rally was it.

Even though I had never driven under extreme snowy or icy conditions, I was thrilled with the idea of driving in the

Monte and didn't have to think twice. A friend of my father, who had some experience of driving in France, sat down with me with very detailed maps of the journey I was about to undertake, which quite honestly meant nothing to me. I tried to be polite and follow what he was saying but my mind was already on the road.

In early January 1962 Sally Anne sent me an airline ticket for the flight from Dublin to Heathrow. I arrived in London to find an immaculately dressed chauffeur standing there with my name on a placard to meet me, something I had only ever seen in films. Outside the airport, we got into a Rolls-Royce and I sat silently in the back of the car, being transported to somewhere in Hertfordshire. I wondered if it was all a dream – maybe I was being kidnapped. I think it only hit me as we drove through the English countryside that I was away from Ireland, all alone and in unfamiliar territory.

It was getting dark by the time we arrived at the house, and as we drove up to the big, imposing mansion my first thought was that there must be a lot of money in fly spray. Sally Anne's father was a lovely English gentleman. He was so kind and put me at my ease as he showed me to my room. The bedroom was luxurious – all pink, with long white drapes at the window overlooking the gardens. He said how good I was to take the drive and explained that this was Sally Anne's last fling before her marriage. As I put down my little case, Mr Cooper informed me that dinner would be at 7.30 p.m. and added, 'We dress for dinner.'

Dress for dinner! I had no evening dress with me and the best clothes I had were on my back. I was wearing a smart grey and white herringbone tweed suit with a long jacket and trousers, which I had made myself. When I confessed that I had no dress, he reassured me and said not to worry about it, I would do fine as I was.

But I was worried; I wanted to make a good impression. I had a quick bath, put on some make-up and had to try to look my best in the tweed trousers and a blouse to wear to dinner. I was young and slim, with long blonde hair, and must have looked well but I certainly wasn't dressed appropriately as I realised immediately when I went downstairs and met Sally Anne for the first time. She was wearing a pale blue taffeta dress and all the men were in dinner jackets with bow ties. I don't know what they made of the Irish girl dressed in trousers and a frilly blouse, but it was too late to worry about that.

Sally Anne's father had bought her a Sunbeam Rapier; it was one of the Rootes' ex-works cars, which I had never driven before. A two-door, four-seater saloon, it had a chunky look about it. It occurred to me much later that Mr Cooper must have been a friend of Lord Rootes to get that ex-works car. The next day we set off on our journey to Scotland. We were headed for Blythswood Square in Glasgow because the Monte Carlo Rally started from various locations and Glasgow was one of them. In those days the Rally started at points all over Europe and converged on Grenoble, then on to Monte Carlo.

I found the Rapier very heavy going at first but I soon got used to it. My social skills not being the greatest, the prospect of having to sit with strangers in the car for 600 kilometres was harder to cope with than driving a Rapier for the first time. On the way we collected Pat Wright, a friend of Sally Anne, who was to be my co-driver. I had never met her before but was relieved to discover that she was easy to talk to and I liked her from the start.

Sixty-five cars left Glasgow to face the long drive down through England to Dover. Pat sat beside me navigating and Sally Anne sat in the back of the car, dressed in a mink coat and red leather gloves, a picnic basket by her side, as she waved to the crowds. She didn't do any driving the whole time we were on that rally.

We drove down to Dover, crossed the English Channel and drove north into Holland and Belgium and then back down into France and over the Alps. I had never encountered snow and ice like that before; I thought the Tim Healy Pass in Kerry was challenging, but this was a whole new ball game. Determined not to let myself down, I found to my amazement that all that slipping and sliding in the big, wet field in Dublin, where my father had taught me to drive, had been excellent training for handling icy roads.

The going was slow, but we made it to Monaco three days later. The sun was shining and we stretched ourselves on the harbour wall. Very soon, a Rolls-Royce came to collect Sally Anne and she said that she would send the car back for us, which she did after what seemed an age. The

Coopers had a beautiful villa in the South of France, just outside Monte Carlo, and when we were eventually picked up we were shown to our rooms at the top of the house, which must have been the servants' quarters. Servants' quarters or not, now that the long drive was over this was like a magical holiday; I enjoyed every minute.

The first thing I did was to buy myself an evening dress to wear and Pat Wright helped me with that. This was my first time in Monte Carlo and I didn't know what to expect. There were awards ceremonies and everything and everybody looked so glamorous. To see Princess Grace for the first time in her dark glasses beside her husband, Prince Rainier III, giving out the trophies was something to tell my mother about when I got home. Mixing with all the other rally drivers, who before this had just been names, was exciting; I didn't know at the time that I would be teammates with some of them before too long.

It was on Saturday night, when we had dinner in the Hotel de Paris, that I met Norman Garrad for the first time. He must have been around 60 years old, and when he approached me I tried to ignore him – I was more interested in talking to the young men of my own age and there were plenty of them around. Norman was the competitions manager for Rootes and in his day had been a force to be reckoned with, giving Stirling Moss and Sheila van Damm their first drives in rallying. But to me, knowing none of this at the time, he was just an annoying elderly man and I couldn't wait to get away from him. When he did manage to get my attention, he offered me the chance to drive on the Rootes' rally team. But I laughed at him. I made it clear that I wasn't interested and shoved his business card in my bag and went on dancing. Norman shrugged his shoulders and, with a knowing smile, moved on. I had no idea that his offer was a chance of a lifetime.

CHAPTER 5

REVVING UP
WITH ROOTES

WHEN I GOT back to Dublin I told my dad about meeting
Norman Garrad and how I had refused his offer of working
for him. My father never usually got annoyed, but this time
he was furious and asked me, did I realise what an honour it
was to have been asked to drive for Rootes? He told me that
the Rootes Group was a famous British car manufacturer
and a major motor dealer business, with offices in the West
End of London and plants in the Midlands and the south of
England. I realised from his reaction that maybe I should
have paid Mr Garrad's proposal a little more attention.

A few months later I received a letter from the Rootes
Group, telling me that they were delighted that I was taking
up Norman Garrad's offer to join the team. My mother
explained that she had written to Rootes' headquarters in
London, telling them that I had changed my mind and would
be available to join them. My parents insisted this was a
chance of a lifetime and I soon realised they were probably
right.

Apparently, Norman Garrad had been behind me on the road when I was driving for Sally Anne, and a friend since told me that he is quoted in *The Rally-Go-Round* by Richard Garrett as saying: 'She was pressing on very smartly and appeared to be the only one alive in the car. I stayed behind her for about two hours, by which time I realised that she had more than average ability.' Norman was a shrewd and experienced businessman and saw the advantage of having this long-legged Irish girl sitting on the bonnet of one of his cars, or, even better, doing the driving. I was often referred to as the 'blonde bombshell'. In his eyes, I was a dolly bird and potentially a great marketing tool too.

The aim of car manufacturers is to sell cars, and rallying and racing was one of the ways to get their message across: a pretty woman adorning their cars was always a help. One of Norman's publicity stunts was to put my name down for Le Mans one year. The 24 Heures du Mans is one of the most prestigious automobile races in the world and on the entry list I was 'R. Smith' driving a Sunbeam Alpine. Norman knew full well that women weren't allowed to drive in the race because in 1956 Annie Bousquet, an Austrian-born French driver, was killed in an accident when she lost control of her Porsche 550 in the early stages of the 12 Heures de Reims. The negative publicity and public outcry caused the French motorsport authorities to prohibit women from entering major races, and the Automobile Club de l'Ouest, organisers of the Le Mans 24

Heures, banned female drivers from competing in their race. Yet previously, in June 1955, a disaster at Le Mans occurred when Pierre Levegh crashed and large fragments of debris flew into the crowd, killing 83 spectators and injuring many more. Despite this appalling accident, the 24 Heures du Mans went on uninterrupted, year after year, but without women drivers.

Norman had arranged everything. I was duly sent for the medical, and when I entered the room the doctor called out 'Smith' and I stepped forward. Not looking at me, he said, 'Drop your trousers.' I gasped and he turned around and looked at me in astonishment. 'You are not a man,' he said. Well spotted, I thought. 'You cannot race. No woman is allowed to race in Le Mans.' The French doctor was a lovely young man, which made my rejection easier to take. The press were all over it and Rootes got loads of publicity, even though none of their cars won that year. In 1971 the French authorities lifted the ban and women were allowed once again to race, but it was too late for me.

Norman Garrad was a very clever man with a weakness for Michelin-starred restaurants. On a recce for the Monte Carlo Rally, when we were preparing pace notes, he would say lunch at 1.30 at such and such a place. It would be out of our way and the crew would protest – it was all right for him, he could just sit there and drink his nice wine but we had work to do. It gets dark very early in January on the continent, and by the time we had this gorgeous lunch the

I made the front page for being a woman

day was over. I remember rally legend Paddy Hopkirk got annoyed and said, 'We are here to practise. Let's have a meal in the evening,' but Norman paid no heed to him. I was only the newcomer and said nothing – in any case I didn't talk back to my elders and betters in those days. Of course, now I would be only too happy to linger over long lunches in Michelin-starred restaurants in France with any well-dressed gentleman who was offering.

Norman was a force to be reckoned with and most of the time I went along with whatever he suggested until an incident in Greece in 1965. We were in Athens a few days before the start of the Acropolis Rally, staying in a hotel right on the beach. The boys in the Rootes team were all going out to dinner and asked me along. Delighted, I was in my room getting dressed when there was a knock on my door and there was Norman. He must have heard that I was going out to dinner with the rest of the crew because when I opened the door he said: 'You needn't think you are going out with the boys. I want you to have dinner with me in my room tonight.' Norman was my boss and I suppose I could have said, 'Yes, of course, I'll stay in and dine with you,' but I didn't. I told the boys what he had said and they told me to come out – I knew I needed the crew on my side if I was to get through the rally.

Furious, Norman said, 'If you don't come to dinner with me, you're sacked and I'm sending you back to London tomorrow.' I went out with the crew anyway and when I came back to my room there was an envelope under my door containing a ticket from Athens to London for the next day. When I told the other drivers, they said to ignore him – 'How would he explain to Lord Rootes why he had sacked you before the rally even began?' they said. So I stayed put and Norman relented and said he would let me stay and do the rally this time. He didn't ask me to dinner again.

When I was with Rootes, I did the Monte about six times, the Scottish and the Geneva Rallies, the Circuit of Ireland and the Tour de France, which wasn't a bicycle race then, most of the time in the Hillman Imp. I loved that little car. Some of the boys were trying to drive the Imp as if it was one of the bigger cars but it was fragile and needed a gentle hand.

The Imp was the first mass-produced British car to have an engine in the back and was a direct competitor to the British Motor Corporation's Mini. They had put it into production in a hurry and it hadn't really been tested properly. Initially, they were falling to pieces when we drove long distances at high speed, and the Imp was never really as fast as the Mini.

I was learning all the time and my good friend Cecil Vard, one of the first Irish drivers to take part in the Monte Carlo Rally, finishing third in 1951, gave me some great advice. He taught me to have the courage to go slowly. Before that I would go flying into a bend, but I eventually saw sense and followed his advice.

Cecil was a talented man, a furrier by trade; he, along with his brothers, Leslie and Jack, owned 'Doreen', manufacturers of ladies' garments in Dublin. All his life he was associated with charitable work and in 1955 he was a founder member and the first president of the Dublin Lions Club. I will always remember his kindness and generosity to me over the years.

I started the 1963 Monte from Paris in a Sunbeam Rapier with my co-driver Rosemary Seers, who Rootes had chosen to drive with me. She worked in London and I didn't know her at all and we had nothing in common. When we were checking in at the start, I noticed that Rosemary was using her left hand to write and her signature was a scrawl. It was then she told me that she had had a slight stroke and she could navigate but wouldn't be able to do much of the driving. When I heard that, I was determined to keep her hands off the steering wheel.

The weather conditions were terrible, and as we left Paris the roads were frozen and it was snowing hard. There were snowdrifts all over Europe that year and the 13 Athens starters didn't make it at all and only 10 of the 59 coming from Glasgow reached Monaco. The snow and ice were bad enough, but fog covered the Alps and I was driving relatively slowly when another rally car came up behind. It was Timo Mäkinen in his Austin Healey and I let him pass. I tucked in behind him, put my foot down and tried to follow, keeping his tail lights in sight as best I could. For a while I lost him and then spotted his tail lights again, but unfortunately he had gone around a hairpin bend. I thought he was straight ahead of me, followed him and we plunged over the edge.

The car rolled over several times on its way down and ended up lodged in a tree. Rosemary Seers was thrown clear of the car; because of her bad arm, she hadn't fixed her seat belt properly. I unstrapped myself and scrambled up the mountainside to the road. The first few cars went straight by and I don't blame them, they were out to win the rally. Eventually, two English-speaking German drivers in a Mercedes stopped. I didn't feel the cold, shock does that, but they quickly placed a rug around me and put me in their car. They scrambled down the slope with a big flashlight, found Rosemary and carried her up to the car. It was only then, as I sat in the back of the car with the unconscious Rosemary beside me, that I got the shakes.

There were no houses nearby and it was a while before they found a farmhouse. An ambulance came and demanded money to take Rosemary to the nearest hospital, which was in Carcassonne, and John Rowe, the PR man from Rootes, drove up and took me on to Monte Carlo. Rosemary had cracked her skull, but luckily I had nothing to show for my trip over the edge of the precipice. It is invariably the co-drivers who get hurt when such accidents happen.

I stayed in the hotel in Monaco and went to the ball on Saturday night, as planned. The next day, John Rowe and I went to Carcassonne to find Rosemary and take her to the American Hospital in Paris. The hospital in Carcassonne hadn't looked after her very well because she had arrived with no money or insurance. Rosemary told us that all she had been given to eat was brown bread and some fish soup. She kept drifting in and out of consciousness but somehow we managed to put her in the car and then on to the train.

It was an overnight trip to Paris, but we had no couchette booked. We laid Rosemary down on one of the long seats in the carriage, but each time the train lurched she fell off and we had to catch her. After this happened several times, we decided to make a bed for her on the floor with our coats and a blanket, where she would be safe, and took ourselves off to the restaurant car.

There was an ambulance waiting for us at the station in Paris to take Rosemary to the hospital, and we went to catch the ferry back to England. She made a full recovery but we never drove together again after that. She should never have come on the rally that year as she was so unwell, but hindsight is a wonderful thing, as they say.

My career with Rootes had begun in earnest and I went on to drive the Hillman Imp in the Monte Carlo Rally many times. In 1964, with Margaret Mackenzie as my co-driver, the run was comparatively trouble-free except for the fog and me being nervous, remembering what had happened in the previous year. Paddy Hopkirk, a brilliant rally driver from Northern Ireland, was the outright winner in 1964 and all the team were so proud of his achievement. Paddy has won the Circuit of Ireland five times, as well as numerous rallies in Europe. He was honoured with an MBE in 2016.

Anyway, as we drove through the gateway of the Prince's Palace of Monaco, there was Princess Grace in a suit of pale green tweed. She looked even more beautiful than in the newspaper pictures or in her films. Along with the other drivers, I was introduced to her and the Irish flag was fluttering in the breeze, although it was 'God Save the Queen' playing in the background. I got the feeling that Princess Grace was delighted to be handing the prize to an Irishman as she greeted Paddy Hopkirk so warmly and with such a lovely smile. I had to make do with a plaque for coming fifth in the Coupe des Dames that year. The Coupe des

Dames was awarded to the Best Female Finisher in the Monte Carlo Rally for the first time in 1927. It is a lady's prize but a certain number of all-female crews had to compete before it could be awarded.

The rich and the famous attend the grand ball held every year in the banqueting hall, wearing fabulous clothes and dancing as the orchestra plays; I feel so lucky to have been part of that.

The next year I drove with Margaret Mackenzie again, and with Valerie Domleo in 1966. Val was terrific – very solid and steady – and she had driven with Pat Moss, sister of Stirling, on a number of occasions. I asked her to be my co-driver and she was very happy to join me and we struck up a good friendship. She was with me when I won the Tulip Rally in 1965 and my co-driver that year in the RAC Rally, the Coupe des Alpes and the Acropolis.

In 1966, 10 cars were disqualified from the Monte Carlo Rally because of so-called faulty headlights. When we were doing practice runs that year in France, we were constantly being told that we had no chance. 'France is going to win this year,' everyone said. 'It's the centenary year.' The French seemed to think it was a foregone conclusion too. When the first three to cross the finishing line were Timo Mäkinen and Rauno Aaltonen from Finland, and Paddy Hopkirk from Ireland, all driving BMC Minis, the Federation Internationale de l'Automobile in Paris said the iodine quartz headlights fitted on the British cars were not standard. Paddy Hopkirk said it was a bit like saying that

because you put a red roof on your car instead of a green one, you were disqualified. Pauli Toivonen, a Finn in a French Citroën, was declared the winner. Toivonen wasn't happy because he rightly felt that it was a wrong decision.

I had won the Coupe des Dames and was disgusted when I was disqualified because the women who were pronounced the winners hadn't even finished. They were all French, of course, and driving French cars. Prince Rainier, who had always been there in previous years, was so angry about it that he left the rally without attending the prize-giving. I

71

said at the time that I would never do another Monte Carlo Rally, but of course I did.

I drove with Valerie Domleo again in the 1967 Monte. Unfortunately, that drive was not a good one for us. We were lying way up front and as we came down the icy mountain road it was snowy and I was going fast. Suddenly, the car skidded and I hit the hub of the back right-hand wheel against the rocks and it shattered, leaving me with only three wheels on my wagon. That was a big disappointment but it was my own fault, I was just going too fast. We had to keep going as it was a very narrow gorge and we limped along until we were able to stop at the widest part so that other cars could pass.

In the 1968 Monte, I drove the Sunbeam Imp with Margaret Mackenzie. A very bright girl, with an upper-class English accent, like many of the girls in the business at that time, she was very competent and usually a great navigator. I had driven with her before in the 1964 Geneva Rally in a Sunbeam Tiger, a sports car with a big engine that I loved. I only got to drive it once – the big cars were almost always kept for the boys. We were going well until Margaret made an error on the outskirts of Geneva, directing us into heavy city traffic. Still, we made it to the finish; only 38 of the 74 starters managed that.

I did well in most of the rallies I took part in, winning the Coupe des Dames many times, but to beat the men outright was something I dreamt about. Sometimes dreams come true and competing in the Tulip Rally in 1965 was one of those times. The whole Rootes team were taking part in the Tulip, one of the big events of our rally year, and again I was to drive the Hillman Imp.

The first Tulip Rally (Tulpenrallye), organised by the Royal Automobile Club of the Netherlands, took place in 1949. It began as an attempt by the Dutch to increase tourism, but over the years became an interesting opportunity for a drive in April/May in comparatively good weather. But 1965 was different: the weather was atrocious.

One hundred and eighty cars began the rally that year. It was a 2,911 km drive through the Netherlands, Belgium, Luxembourg, Germany and France as part of the European Championship. Richard Burton, who was in Holland filming *The Spy Who Came in from the Cold*, waved us off to begin the drive through 19 special stages, 84 checks, as well as special tests. Due to the snow, however, several of the tests were cancelled and only 45 competitors finished the event, the lowest completion rate ever. My teammates Peter Harper and Peter Riley, in their two big Sunbeam Tigers, were among those who were forced to drop out. The trek from Noordwijk and back again saw some of the worst weather ever experienced at that time of the year and many of the cars were left stranded in the snow. This proved to be to the advantage of Tiny Lewis, who came second, and myself, with the biggest handicap, both of us driving a Hillman Imp.

The Imp was like a toy car compared to the Tigers and the Austin-Healey 3000 that the Morley brothers drove

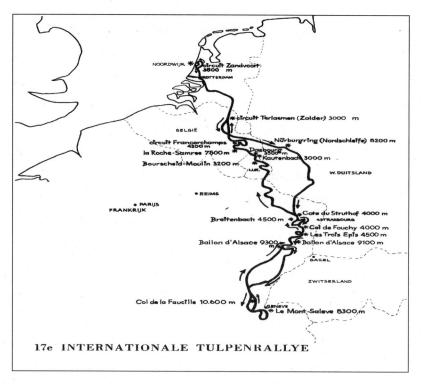

Map of the Tulip route 1965

and the Cortina of Eric Jackson, but it was light and managed the snow and ice so much better than the bigger cars, although at one point Valerie Domleo, my co-driver, had to get out of the car, sit on the boot lid and bounce up and down to get traction to ascend a particularly slippery part of one of the mountain passes. Poor Val, when she got back in the car it took ages for her hands to thaw out and tears were running down her face – she was marvellous! Rod Waller, an Australian cartoonist, sent me a cartoon of Valerie sitting on the back of the car in a block of ice, so news must have spread far and wide of that endeavour.

We got stuck at one stage and the car just would not shift. As so often happened, the voice of my father was in my ears: 'If you can't move, get the mats out of the car and put them under the wheels.' I had no mats, but I did have a beautiful suede jacket that I had bought in Spain, so I pushed it in under the back wheels and it worked. Then I sailed off, leaving other drivers pushing and pulling at their cars.

Exhausted by the end of that rally, Valerie and I retired to our room in the beautiful hotel in Noordwijk to have a well-deserved rest. I knew we had done well to get around the road section clean and that we had recorded good times on the speed tests, but until the complicated marking was completed no one knew anything for certain. As we lay on our beds, there was a frantic knocking on the door and

someone was yelling for us to get up and come downstairs immediately. We wondered what the matter was, but took no notice and didn't move until someone else knocked again and told us we had won. We had won the Tulip Rally and didn't even realise it!

Richard Burton and Elizabeth Taylor were staying at the same hotel and sent me a bouquet of flowers and a lovely letter, which, unfortunately, is no longer in my possession. I lent it to someone to photograph but it was never returned.

In Ireland, my win was reported in the news and my photo appeared on the front page of *The Irish Times* on 1 May 1965, the caption reading: 'Miss Rosemary Smith of Dublin who was declared official winner of the international Tulip Rally in Noorwijk, Holland last night'. When I got back to Ireland later that month, a Hillman Imp went on a promotional tour around the country and I drove the last section from Cork to Dublin.

The Coupe des Alpes, or the Alpine Rally, as the British call it, is a punishing event as only half an hour's lateness means exclusion. If anything goes wrong with your car, it is very unlikely that you will be able to continue. You have to drive up and down those roads in the Alps as fast as you possibly can and just hope the car doesn't give trouble. Drivers tend to retire, especially in the first few hours, when any fault the car may possess usually comes to light.

The Alpine Rally was one of the most gruelling motoring events I ever undertook. It is run over some of the most demanding tarmac and gravel roads in the world and is a challenge for the most experienced of drivers. I drove in the Coupe des Alpes in 1963, 1965, 1966 and 1967. It went on day and night, no stopping for a rest, driving all the time around the hairpin bends, with horrendous drops over the side.

On one occasion as we came round a bend, I saw some pace notes on the road – obviously the navigator had let them fall out of the car. We got up to the next hairpin, and as we passed I saw a glove on the ground and I swear it was moving, sort of twitching, as it opened and closed. When we got to the top of the pass, the whole rally was stopped and the story was that one of the works' Lancias had gone off the road, rolled down on a culvert and come out on the road below. The co-driver had his hand out of the window and as the car turned over his hand was amputated at the wrist.

It was on the same rally that my back wheel came off. 'This is it, we're out,' my co-driver, Margaret Mackenzie, said to me as we ground to a halt. We saw the wheel careering down the incline and I clambered down and retrieved it; the donut had broken, which they did at regular intervals with the Imp. When he saw our predicament, a farmer came down the road from his house, yattering away in French. He managed to get the wheel back on with the help of nails and bits of metal that stuck out of the middle of the wheel, making the car look most peculiar. Although we ended up a bit late, we got to the final control by chugging along not on the road but on the promenade in Cannes, scattering people and dogs everywhere.

At the end of the rally, the mechanics took the offending piece off the car, nails and all, had it silvered and made into the most beautiful plaque, which they presented to me some months later in London. The competition manager had said give up (he should have known better), the mechanics knew I wouldn't, and they must have been proud of my determination. Inscribed were the words: 'To the girls who kept it going from the mechanics who tried to keep it going'. It was the trophy that meant the most to me and I was heartbroken when it was recently stolen from my house in Sandyford, along with all my silver jewellery. Why anyone would want that trophy is quite beyond me.

That farmer was a lifesaver, and spectators can be very useful, once they don't get in the way. On one of those Alpines, Anne Hall, who was a really lovely lady and a very good driver, approached one of the many very twisty parts of the pass at a fierce rate and went right over the edge, landing at the bottom of a rocky gorge. I looked down and could see a crowd of people around her. 'That's one of our opposition gone,' I said to Margaret. But I was wrong, because the spectators scrambled down and pushed her up a very steep incline, back on the road and, by some miracle, got her going again.

People are fanatical about rallying and will stand for hours watching the cars go by. In every country, the spectators and supporters are amazing. They come out of farmhouses to help if you need them; some stand on the side of the road, waving and cheering, which is lovely but if you are in a mad rush and there are hundreds of people in the way it can slow you down. You go out to win, and despite notices everywhere saying, 'Warning to the Public: Motor Racing is Dangerous' and 'You are here at your own risk', people will stand on the very edge of roads and get in the way. Sometimes, unfortunately, they get hurt.

Driving in the Monte, the Tulip and all the other rallies in Europe was great. I had so many new experiences and met some wonderful people, but nothing prepared me for what I would find on the other side of the Atlantic. In the early 1960s the Rootes Group were in financial difficulties and were encountering industrial relations problems in the UK. In 1964 Rootes began to be taken over in stages by the Chrysler Corporation, while I was still under contract. It seemed Rootes and Chrysler thought that the Sunbeam Alpine was a car that would suit the American market and that I would look good behind the wheel for promotion purposes.

CHAPTER 6

THE AMERICAS

I WAS ASKED by Rootes/Chrysler to drive in the 24-hour endurance race in Daytona, Florida. They wanted to promote the Sunbeam and what better way than to have glamorous women drivers behind the wheel! Our sponsors were Macmillan Ring Free Motor Racing Oil and we were given the title of 'Motor Maids'. When I look back on it now, calling us Motor Maids was so demeaning. It made us sound as if we were servant girls, but it was the 1960s and feminism had no place in the motor industry's agenda.

I flew to New York in January 1966, and was met by John Norwood, the PR guy for Macmillan. Naturally, I was expecting to fly down to Florida, but John had different ideas. He brought me out to his old beat-up Citroën and said, 'We're driving. I need the car in Florida.' He had a big muffler and a heavy coat. 'I hope you have something warm to wear. There's no heater in the car,' he added.

We drove 1,000 miles and it took us over 15 hours. What with the jet lag, that awful drive and the cold, I was exhausted. When we arrived, I told the Macmillan people that I needed to get to bed. 'I'm shattered after that long drive,' I told them. 'What drive?' they asked. They couldn't believe it because they had given John air tickets for the journey. It wasn't the best of starts.

There were two all-female teams comprising the Motor Maids: Janet Guthrie, Donna Mae Mims, Suzy Dietrich, Smokey Drolet and myself. Janet was a pilot, flight instructor and aerospace engineer, there was talk that she was going to be the first woman to go into space; Donna Mae Mims was known as 'Think Pink' because she had pink hair, pink overalls, pink everything; Suzy Dietrich, a librarian, was married to a racing driver; and then there was Smokey Drolet, who in 1960 won the Nassau Ladies' Race in the Bahamas, driving a Daimler SP25. She was to be my co-driver.

The Americans were trying to make the Daytona 24-hour endurance race like the Le Mans event in France. But how could they? Le Mans was held in France, in June, when the sun was shining and the course was on public roads – closed, of course, to all other traffic. The Daytona took place in February and is conducted on a closed course – it was actually a speedway arena, with high banks intended for stock cars and not fragile cars, like the Alpine I was driving.

There was a fast infield section that included two hairpins and a sharp double bend on the back straight. Along the pit lane, crews put up plastic curtains to protect them from the freezing wind, which looked pretty at night with the lights shining, but when daylight came the area resembled a shanty town. The 24 hours of driving in Daytona took in the freezing night, sunrise, blue skies and sunshine. It was a real survival test for me and the car. The surface of the track was bumpy, the Alpine's suspension took a pounding, and by the end of it I felt as if I had done three rounds with Muhammad Ali.

Smokey and I took it in turns to drive the full of the petrol tank and then we swapped over. There was a caravan at the back of the pits, where we could go for a rest and wait our turn to start again. As we were driving the Sunbeam Alpine, which had a small engine, we were told to keep in the first two lanes of the banking. We could see the headlights of the much faster cars approaching from behind us in the distance and then whoosh! They were upon us and away again. We were only doing about 110 mph, while they were driving at 200 mph, and they would speed past in a flash. It was scary at times, and although I had to concentrate I found it monotonous driving round and round those 200 laps so I started picking off my nail polish out of sheer boredom. Holding the steering wheel in one hand, I would pull off my glove with my teeth and start picking away at the polish, which fell on the floor of the car.

When the car came into the pit stop for refuelling the mechanics thought something was very wrong when they saw the coloured scrapings on the floor – rust or something, they imagined, and started to investigate. I tried to tell them it was only my nail polish and when I finally managed to get through to them they were not amused. I have always kept my nails painted and long – still do, although people don't believe they are my own. I wore false eyelashes too; my make-up and clothes have always been an important part of my image, in or out of a car. The false eyelashes were a great help at times as, when I got very tired and my eyelids started to droop, the lashes would come down like a fringe, tickling my cheeks and making sure I didn't drift off.

Once it started to get light, the crowds gathered to watch and things got a little more interesting. There were 59 starters in that race and only 32 finished. Smokey and I came 30th overall and the other American girls were last, in 32nd place.

Daytona was held on 6 February 1966, and a week later I appeared on *What's My Line?* in New York, which was broadcast live by CBS. The Chrysler and Macmillan people had managed to get me on the show as another way to advertise their cars.

What's My Line? was a panel game show watched by everyone in America in the 1960s. There was a team of celebrity panellists who questioned contestants in order to determine what their occupations were. When I came on, I wrote on a blackboard my job, which was, in American terms, an 'Automobile Race Driver'. The audience showed their surprise at the contrast between my appearance and my job. I was wearing a beautiful turquoise suit with a marabou feather trim, which I had made myself, and my bouffant hairstyle and make-up were perfect. When I watch that broadcast on YouTube today, I can see that I did look the part and the Irish accent probably helped, but inside I was dying.

One of the celebrity panellists was Ginger Rogers, the famous actress and dancer who often partnered Fred Astaire, and who was currently appearing in *Hello, Dolly!* on Broadway. Another of the panellists asked if I was in show business and when I told him no, he said I should be, and Ginger Rogers asked me to join her in *Hello, Dolly!* But I can honestly say that hearing those compliments and praise for my appearance meant nothing to me.

When driving I was confident and self-assured, but all that was left behind when I got out of the car. People often got the idea that I was stand-offish because I had nothing to say, but the truth is, I was shy. When meeting people, who I assumed were so much more intelligent than me, I felt embarrassed at my lack of education. Today I embrace everything and anything with enthusiasm, but that's what life experience has given me. Put me in front of a television camera now and I am well able to hold my own, but back then I felt inadequate.

After that appearance on *What's My Line?*, Chrysler took me to Hollywood for more promotional work and I met the actors and directors on set. If only mobile phones and selfies were around then, I could have had pictures of me with Ernest Borgnine, who was a lovely man, the adorable Debbie Reynolds and our own Maureen O'Hara.

Chrysler thought that it would be great publicity for me to drive Bob Hope in a big open-topped car around the mountains behind Universal Studios. Hope sat in the back of the car, his minders either side of him. It was obvious he didn't want to be there any more than I did. I couldn't believe that the funny man I had seen in the films could be so strait-laced and unfriendly. Maybe he had seen too many leggy blondes to get excited about me, no matter how many trophies I had accumulated or how many Montes I had driven.

When I returned to Dublin, my family, delighted with my success in America, wanted to hear all about my adventures.

A drink with Maureen O'Hara in Universal Studios

I had hoped to spend some time with them and recharge my batteries, but it was not to be. Soon enough, I was summoned to the Rootes factory in Coventry to begin preparation for the Shell 4000, a rally from Vancouver to Quebec, which was to take place from 30 April to 6 May that same year, 1966. Shell was Rootes' fuel-supplying sponsor, so entry was a given. In the Shell 4000 rally competitors were allowed 15 minutes at the end of each day to carry out essential repairs without assistance from anyone.

Des O'Dell, Rootes' head mechanic, wanted me to learn about the inside of the Imp engine to prepare me for any emergencies. He stood beside me and told me how to take out every part of the engine. I did that all right but when I had to put them back I was totally lost. I tried and tried to

Bob Hope and film crew

get it right, but I hadn't a clue about engines – still don't to this day. In the end, Des put coloured tape around the wires and stuck an instruction sheet on the inside of the boot lid. It read: If such and such happens, put the blue wire to the red and the green to the yellow, and so on. That wasn't such a great start, but despite my lack of mechanical knowledge we did well in Canada.

There were over 60 entries that year and only 26 completed the course; I was one of them, winning the Coupe des Dames. As soon as that little Imp rolled off the starting ramp, I was always out to win and I especially enjoyed beating the men. By the second day we were in the running for the Coupe des Dames, but that was never my aim: I wanted to be in the overall results. The Imp was great at tackling the icy, winding mountain roads over the Rockies. While the bigger cars had to make several attempts to get around the hairpin bends, the Imp did it first time on the handbrake.

My navigator, Anne Coombe, was an Englishwoman living in Canada. Anne was a very good navigator and I should have been happy to have her beside me. The only thing was she insisted on wearing wellington boots in the car and, as time went by, they got smellier and smellier. I have a sensitive nose at the best of times and it really annoyed me; mind you, those boots did come in handy when we got stuck in the mud outside Ottawa.

In May the following year we entered again. This time 93 cars left the starting ramp in Vancouver, but only 43

Mum, Dad and Boy

Attempt at being an
actress at school

Dad and I in 1950

Dad and Roger

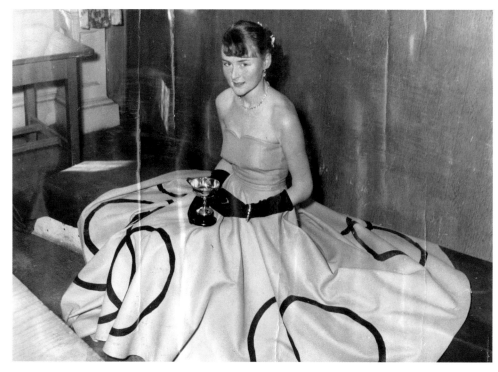

Winner, Grafton Academy, Student of the Year 1953

Pamela, her husband Sean, my father and I

My entrée into car racing: First in Class 1 Championship

Frank Bigger, my mentor in motor sport, racing in 1954

My first hill-climb car, lent to me by Billy Lacey, who had won the Circuit of Wicklow

Test Trial in Frank Bigger's car: a Triumph Herald

My Lotus Elan at Brands Hatch before I wrote it off

With my co-drivers Pat Wright and Sally Anne Cooper, Monte Carlo 1962

Prize-giving with
my then co-driver,
Rosemary Seers, on
Coupes des Alpes

Coupes des Alpes 1963

Margaret Mackenzie and I with the
Sunbeam Tiger on the Geneva Rally

The RAC Rally, our first
event out of Ireland for
Delphine and me

Valerie Domleo and I in the Hillman Imp on our way to winning the International Tulip Rally

Promotional photograph at Rootes' Head Office in Devonshire House, London, with Pamela after the Tulip Rally

Flowers, flowers and more flowers!

Snow was everywhere on the Monte Carlo Rally, January 1965

And even more snow on the 1966 Monte Carlo Rally

Driving a Porsche on the Geneva Rally 1968 with Ginette de Rolland when our brake pipes were cut

You meet all sorts on rallies!

Start of the Shell 4000 with Anne Coombe, co-driver

Water, water everywhere! Being pushed out of it on the Shell 4000 Rally in Canada

made it to Montreal. The going was rough: thick mud, blinding dust in the prairies, pelting rain and clinging snow. At one stage, as we approached Espanola in Northern Ontario, the water was so deep, we sank; luckily, the Canadian Mounties were there to push us out. In those situations it is handier to drive a light car, like the Imp, because it is easier to lift and move.

Disaster struck when we were coming along a gravel track and Anne said we were forking off on to a main road, but she didn't tell me there was a six-foot drop and we just went flying. The Imp took off into the air and, with the engine in the rear, the front wheels came down hard and twisted outwards. Luckily, there were no other cars on the highway at the time. We limped along until we met up with Des, who instructed me to drive off the road at a certain point. He had seen a big old barn ahead and wanted to get me in there to see what he could do – strictly against the rules, of course.

When we straggled into the barn, lo and behold, there was another women's team having repairs done on their car. They looked shocked when they saw our little tin box with its wheels all askew. But I knew they wouldn't report us – after all, we were both in the same boat, or should I say, barn? Des tried, but couldn't do much to straighten the wheels, and so we carried on at a slow pace. I think he thought we wouldn't make it, but I was determined to finish. I noticed there was a big red Pontiac behind us and only later learned that the car contained officials, making sure no repairs were made to cars along the way. They hadn't caught us going into the barn. Luck was on our side.

Outside Montreal on the last day the rain was pelting down and a motorcycle police escort took us into the stadium, but we couldn't keep up with them. Despite everything, when we eventually arrived I stepped out of the car in my shocking pink suit to learn that we were 13th overall, and once again we had won the Coupe des Dames.

I loved Canada and America and all the razzmatazz but didn't get a chance to return until March 1969, to compete in the 12 Hours of Sebring. No Palm Beach, Sebring is a small town in the centre of Florida. Like most of Florida, it is flat, drab and full of lakes and swamps. Apart from a few motels and guest houses, there is nothing much going on. It only comes to life once a year for Sebring, the 12-hour endurance race held in a disused World War II army airfield. The race starts during the day and finishes at night. Thousands of spectators come from all over the States, a lot of them college boys on spring break.

I was picked up by one of the women team drivers at the airport. She, let's call her Susan, put me in the front seat beside her and there were two of her friends in the back of the car. Susan chatted away, telling me about her prowess as a driver and all that she had achieved, and as I turned around to include the women behind me in the conversation I saw that they were snogging and had no interest in what we were talking about. I like to think that I am as broad-minded as the next person and behaved as if this was nothing out of the ordinary.

When we arrived at the guest house, I was tired and ready for bed. It was a nice little place, all wood and lace curtains. Susan and I were sharing a bedroom and she insisted I use the bathroom first. I was surprised when I came out of the bathroom in my nightdress to see that Susan had pushed the beds together. I was even more surprised when she emerged from the bathroom some time later, stark naked. I am not a lover of the human body unclothed, male or female, and I was shocked.

'Oh, honey,' she said, 'it's much too hot to wear anything. Take that off.' Take it off? At that stage I was only short of putting my driving suit on for protection. Why does it always happen to me? I don't give out signals, at least I don't think I do, but many women have propositioned me over the years.

We drove a BMW 2002 that year. Of the 70 cars that started, only 47 finished and we were among them. Many of the drivers of the fast sports cars, like the Ferraris, Alfa Romeos and Porsches, drove their machines so hard that they never made it to the finish, but we were not out to break records, just to reach home.

I did Sebring again the next year, in 1970, and drove with Janet Guthrie and Judy Kondratieff, this time in a lovely Austin Healey, affectionately known as a 'Frogeye' Sprite because its headlights are prominently mounted on top of the bonnet. Steve McQueen, the highest-paid movie star of the 1970s, who was an avid motor racing enthusiast, drove a Porsche with his left leg in a plaster cast, asbestos wrapped around it so that it wouldn't melt. Amazingly, he came second to Mario Andretti in a Ferrari.

The last time I went to Sebring was in 1971, with Janet again and this time a Scottish girl, Jennifer Birrell, but it was a disaster. Janet Guthrie was the first to drive. I had made the best time in practice and it is usually the custom for the fastest to start the race, but because Janet was the American she was first to go. We were driving a Chevron B16 and I was so excited to be driving something that could really move for a change.

It was on the first lap when it happened: after the start and finish line you come down to a sharp right hairpin bend, and instead of taking the turn she went straight on into a sandbank. This was a 12-hour race and the car had a rear engine. Had she just turned the engine off, the marshals could have pushed her out. But Janet put the car into reverse, revved the engine, sucked in sand through the air vents in the front and the engine blew up on the spot. When I say I was annoyed, that is an understatement, but there was nothing I could do about it. I never even got a chance to get behind the wheel of that Chevron, and that was one of the biggest disappointments of my motor racing career.

My experiences in America and Canada had been challenging in many respects. That's the way it goes in life, especially in the motor racing and rallying business: you have your triumphs and disasters, you win some, you lose some, but I loved it all.

I had begun a relationship with a man in Ireland, who was to become my husband, but because of my career the days I spent with him were limited. I was always away from home. We lived together, which was not the done thing in those days, and my mother didn't approve. He wasn't good enough for me, she said, but I paid no heed.

CHAPTER 7

AVOIDABLE ACCIDENTS

I WAS ALWAYS happy driving, but over the course of my career, and my personal life, I have had, like most people, many ups and downs, which I dealt with as best I could. Behind the wheel I was in my element; it didn't matter to me what I was driving – it could be a racing car, a big saloon, a go-kart or my little Imp. When I was rallying, the Imp was great on the corners and I would nip around the bends, but then the men came along in their big cars, passed me on the hills and I would be left behind; in my car with its small engine even the downhills were up.

There came a stage in my career when I had won many rallying events and was tempted to give racing a go. In those days racing was almost an exclusively male sport but that didn't put me off. Some people were of the opinion that women shouldn't participate at all. There was always a big divide between racing and rallying and some of the men said, anybody can rally, you have to race to prove yourself. Even in rallying, it was difficult for some of my teammates to accept me and it wasn't until I started to win consistently that they came to realise I wasn't just a dumb blonde.

Peter Procter was the exception – he was always my champion from the beginning. I think he realised that if I had been given the chance to drive a decent car I would have been even more successful. Peter's racing career ended in 1966, when he was hit from behind in a saloon car race at Goodwood. The impact burst the petrol tank and the car flew into the air and somersaulted several times. He had no broken bones and leapt out of the car in flames, sustaining third-degree burns to 65 per cent of his body.

My mother and I adored him, and when she heard the news she telephoned me. When I went to see him the following week, in the Burns Unit of the Queen Victoria Hospital in East Grinstead, Sussex, all I could do was stare at him through a glass window as he lay there, covered in bandages. I never thought he would survive that horrendous accident, but he did due to the team of Sir Archibald McIndoe, who had pioneered experimental plastic surgery on airmen disfigured by burns in World War II. Motorsport is still dangerous today, but in those days the safety standards were primitive. I was delighted to meet Peter and his wife, Shirley, at the Stoneleigh Motor Show recently.

The first racing car I bought was a Lotus Elan; my pride and joy, it cost me all of £2,000. One Christmas I took it to the Brands Hatch Circuit in Kent to practise for the annual Boxing Day event. There were about 30 cars in the race, I was third on the grid and the weather had deteriorated dramatically. In Brands Hatch you come down under a tunnel and out onto the track itself, and as I was going around on the warm-up lap to get in line the car hit ice, spun off the track and hit the bank. I was left sitting there, dazed, with the steering wheel in my hand, fibreglass and bits of car all over the place. I'm not even sure I had four wheels left.

It was a practice run for the first race of the event and it was obvious that nobody had gone out to inspect the track. There was so much ice that I don't know how anybody got around it, or even if they did. I heard that Jonathan Mills, the actor John Mills's son, who was driving a Jaguar, went over the finishing line backwards. I had to bow out and swallow my pride.

Rootes lent me a car, and because no bones were broken I thought I would be all right. I was due to go to Sweden that evening for a televised ice race which the BBC were going to film and there was no way I was going to miss that. Pat Moss was driving in the event and I wanted to be there and, who knows, maybe beat her.

I got into the car in Kent and drove to Harwich, where I was to get the boat to the Hook of Holland. To this day I don't know how I got there; I have no recollection of that drive whatsoever. All the other cars were there at the Harwich docks, and when the other drivers saw the state I was in they brought me to be examined by a doctor, who pronounced that I had concussion and three cracked ribs.

I was told to go home, but as is so typical of me I insisted that I would be grand.

It was a seven-hour journey on the boat and I decided that if I had a good rest all would be well – although by this time every bone in my body was aching. I got into the bunk bed and after a couple of hours' sleep I tried to get up, but I couldn't: I had totally stiffened up. The cabin was tiny and I just managed to get the door open and shout for help. A passer-by came in and helped me get out of the bed. I was just about able to get off the boat and drive to the Saab training headquarters where we were to stay, and it was there that another of the many strange episodes I have had with a woman occurred.

I arrived at the headquarters in a state of collapse and was immediately taken under the wing of a very large Swedish lady, who appeared to be in charge and who could see I was in distress. She was most concerned about my injuries and helped me undress and ran a hot bath for me. All the fuss and attention she gave me was just what I needed, but at the same time I sensed something wasn't quite right. After dinner that evening, in my bedroom I found a red rose on the pillow. I locked my door and when she came knocking I pretended to be asleep. Next morning I thought I was ready for anything.

The ice race was held on a frozen lake in the grounds of the Saab training school and the temperature was below freezing. I was driving the Imp and all the cars were fitted with special studded tyres to provide better traction and increased speed. Ice racing featured in one of the James Bond films, *On Her Majesty's Secret Service*, with 007 (George Lazenby) trying to escape his pursuers.

Determined to do well, I started off in great style with the BBC cameras all around. I was catching the car ahead when suddenly I started to slip and slide. Completely out of control, I went towards the stand where the BBC cameramen were filming. The impact of the car toppled the stand, and cameras, cameramen and all their equipment ended up in deep, powdery snow. Enthusiasm had overcome my better judgement and of course anyone with a bit of sense would know that I should never have gone to Sweden in that condition at all. Not one of my better decisions, I'm afraid. I went home and spent two weeks in bed, waiting for my body to return to normal.

Racing you do alone, but rallying is a two- or three-person job. Navigators and co-drivers can make a big difference to how things turn out in rallies. Valerie Domleo was not the only navigator whom I have called upon to go beyond the call of duty. Pauline Gullick, still my good friend after all our ups and downs, was navigating for me in a Lotus Sunbeam on the Donegal rally one time. I could feel there was something wrong with the throttle cable going through the bulkhead, and when we went into the control I told the mechanic, an ex-driver who didn't like me, and the feeling was mutual. I explained that the cable was catching going through the bulkhead and every time I pressed down on the accelerator I had to put my foot in under the pedal to yank it back up again. He tut-tutted away, as if I was talking rubbish, looked inside at the engine, did some banging around with a spanner and said it was fixed.

The minute I started up the road I knew it wasn't right, but then, of course, we had to keep going. Eventually, the cable frayed and snapped and I was left with no acceleration. There was nothing for it: Pauline clambered on to the wing and pressed the accelerator down with her thumb. She sat under the bonnet with her legs dangling over the wing. The bonnet was up so it was very difficult for me to steer as I could hardly see where I was going. We were doing 60 mph and she was hanging on when we hit a bump and then another. The bonnet hit the windscreen, and the next I saw of Pauline she was rolling behind me down the road. She was knocked unconscious and it was a good thing she was wearing a helmet because without it she would have been killed. The side of her head was badly grazed, her thumb had been ripped right back and was hanging off.

A few cars passed us and didn't stop because it was a special stage, timed to the last second. Eventually, someone stopped, put her in their car and drove to an ambulance, which took her straight to hospital. All I felt at the time was annoyance that we were out of the event because we had been doing so well: you go out to win and I have been told many times that I took rallying too seriously. How else are you supposed to take it?

Pauline was personal assistant to the governor of the prison in Bristol, and months later she bent down in the office to pick something up and couldn't move. Her back had been broken in that accident and she was on the broad of her back and unable to work for months. Pauline still rallies with Jimmy McRae in historic events and, despite everything, we remain very good friends. She tells me that she met that mechanic recently, when he apologised to her and admitted it had been his fault.

I have been very lucky to have survived my career without serious injury. However, there are occasions when no amount of skill or determination will get you through because things happen over which you have no control. The mechanic who didn't listen to me when I told him the cable was catching in Donegal was at fault and I was also nearly killed in the Monaghan Rally because of the stupidity of another man.

On that overnight rally I was driving a front engine Lotus Sunbeam with Peter Scott as my co-driver. Peter is a very experienced navigator and determined, like myself. It was in the early hours of the morning, pitch-black, and we were doing really well and flying along. Peter was encouraging me to pick up speed as we were on a long, straight stretch of road. It was one of those places that you come across in some parts of Ireland, where there is nothing on either side of the road and it is difficult to see where the road ends and the bogland begins. We were flat out and whipping along when suddenly every light in the car went out. Blackness descended, and before we knew it we were upon a sharp right-hand turn, which in the darkness I couldn't see, and the car just went straight on. The Lotus flew into the air off the road, rolled over and over, and eventually landed on its wheels. All I could hear was Peter roaring and howling – he must have thought we were dead.

It was a notorious bend on that particular rally and soon there were hordes of people around to help us. Some of the lads went back up the road to slow the cars in case they missed the turn and landed straight on top of us. Peter had calmed down by this stage when he realised we weren't hurt. We left the car, got a lift down to a townland called Newbliss and went into the Garda station to let them know what had happened. I told the guard we had left the car up there and we would see to it in the morning, and he replied, 'Oh missus, if I were you I'd go back up there right away, because there'll be nothing left of it by the morning.'

He was right. When it got light we went back to the car and, apart from the engine, everything else was gone: seats, tyres, lights and my precious Halda. To me, the worst thing was the loss of the Halda as it is an expensive instrument which computes time and distance and is invaluable when rallying. After the London to Sydney Marathon in 1968, which I did for Ford, they gave me that Halda and it held great sentimental value.

The mechanics came down and fitted new tyres, but without a seat I was obliged to sit on two spare tyres to drive the car back to Dublin. I gave out hell when I found out afterwards that a man who worked in the car show-room where my car was garaged had taken my car to enter an event the night before the Monaghan Rally. During his drive the alternator had gone. He brought it back to try and repair it, and after fiddling around he thought it was fixed. I was furious, but that was what I was up against a lot of the time. Some men didn't have as much respect or pay attention as they should, because I was a woman!

CHAPTER 8

MOVING ON

BEING A WOMAN had its advantages when publicity was required in various parts of the globe. I didn't hesitate when Chrysler asked me to help promote its cars in Australia, and that's where I met Peter Janson in Melbourne, in 1967. He was one of the most extraordinary men I have ever met. Peter had thick eyebrows, naughty eyes and a jet-black beard, which he said he grew after his jaw was smashed in a racing accident. He was a socialite who had friends in England, India and Northern Ireland and was obviously a man of means, although where he got his money from was a mystery. When asked his occupation, he would say he was a gentleman. I believe his father was the British Ambassador in Mexico or somewhere but he was deliberately vague about his background. He was about the same age as myself when we met, but it was obvious he had seen much more of life than I had.

I was in Melbourne to help David Brown of the Chrysler Motor Company promote cars and Peter Janson was organising publicity. A dinner was arranged for twenty people with Peter acting as mine host and he invited me to sit beside him. The wine, cocktails and champagne flowed during that four-course meal, which included caviar, lobster and oysters. When the dinner was over, Peter clicked his fingers and called for the bill. As I was sitting close to him, I noticed that he took a matchbox from his pocket and very discreetly opened it and put something on the side of his plate under a lettuce leaf. When he got the bill, he pushed the lettuce to one side and lo and behold, there was a slug on his plate. Peter acted surprised and the waiter was horrified. The Maître D' apologised profusely and assured Peter there was no charge for our extravagant dinner.

But the evening wasn't over. Peter invited some of us to go back to his place for yet another drink. We drove off and I was quite taken aback when we got out of the car to find that he lived in a tower. It was a tower that had belonged to the Federal Hotel (now demolished) and had been built initially just for decoration. Peter had seen its potential and had transformed it into an incredible and most bizarre two-storey home.

As we entered the tiny entrance hall, an enormous peach-coloured mirror faced us and then we began the climb up the rosewood staircase. The carpets were all rich gold and red and the porthole windows hung with deep wine-coloured velvet curtains. Each side of the staircase and all along the corridor was filled with photographs of famous women, and Peter assured us he knew them all personally.

The main living room was enormous, with velvet sofas, bric-à-brac of all shapes and sizes, books and lifelike stuffed animals. Drinks were handed around, and as we sipped our drinks the lights became dimmer and a creaking noise came from the side of the room. Along the wall were headstones that started to move, and coffins were opening. It was most macabre. Peter explained that when he was entertaining ladies, hearing the noise and seeing the lids of the coffins move, they would get frightened and jump into his arms!

Up a few steps, like a kind of mezzanine, was the bedroom, under the dome of the tower. There, in the middle of the room, was a huge bed and steps up to it. I politely declined his offer to try it out and he said, 'Look what's on the other side.' When I walked around the bed, I saw a blue tiled sunken bath. It looked most out of place but Peter said he liked to be able to roll out of bed to bathe after – well, you know what. Peter Janson moved out of his tower long ago, but is still alive and entertaining friends in his five-storey mansion, Rutherglen House in Melbourne, and I would love to meet him again.

Meeting Peter was one of the last adventures I had with the Rootes/Chrysler Group. I was on the Rootes' team when I won the Tulip Rally in 1965, and during my time with the company I drove the Rapier, Alpine, Tiger and Imp, and won many Coupe des Dames, class wins and overall placings in over 30 major international events. Norman Garrad retired in 1965, and maybe it was because I was his protégée that I was no longer the flavour of the month. For whatever reason, in 1968 it was decided my services were no longer required.

From then on, away from Chrysler and Rootes, I was freelance, and there was no shortage of offers. Fritz Huschke von Hanstein, Porsche's public relations manager and chief of their racing department, gave me a Porsche 911 to drive in the 1968 Geneva Rally – mainly, I think, because he fancied me. That rally didn't end so well, although at one stage I thought that I was going to make history.

I loved that Porsche; it was a two-door sports car with the engine in the rear, and it was fast. I was driving with Ginette de Rolland, a French girl and a very good navigator. We were lying second overall, catching Pauli Toivonen, also in a Porsche, for the lead, when it happened. It was 3 a.m. and I was doing about 80 mph when Ginette said, 'Slow down, slow down.' She was calling out the pace notes on a special stage and told me that we were coming to a very sharp right-hand bend. I pressed the foot brake and it went straight down to the floor. Once again my father's words came to me: 'If you can't stop with your brakes, drop down through the gears.' Ginette was screaming in my ear, 'Stop, stop!' as I tried to slow the car, but there was nothing I could do. The road was very narrow and on one side there was no wall, just a sheer drop going down into the ravine. We were still going fast and as we approached a sharp right-hand bend I knew we weren't going to stop with no brakes, so I dropped down very quickly through the gears until I got first gear, the car slowed and then I yanked the handbrake and dived the nose of the car into the cliff face.

Ginette wasn't moving and I thought she had been badly hurt. I went around to her side of the car and saw she was vomiting. We waited for the next car to come and they managed to pull the tail of the car into the side of the road so that the oncoming drivers could pass us. I didn't know then that two of Ginette's friends had been killed in an accident at that very spot the year before. We were lucky to get away uninjured.

Porsche learned a lot from that accident because when they examined the car they found that the rear shock absorber had broken and the engine had dropped, severing the brake pipes. I was lucky to be alive, but even so it was a shame really because I thought I could have won and beaten Pauli (nice thought!) and all the other male drivers. It was yet another big disappointment in my career. They picked us up and brought us to Geneva and Ginette's husband came and collected her.

I stayed at the hotel, where I spent a few days in the company of a very handsome Swedish man, who cheered me up no end. I can't remember his name but that doesn't matter, he was gorgeous!

I was enjoying the freedom of being freelance, especially as it meant I could accept Ford's offer to drive in the 1968 London to Sydney Rally. I was off again!

CHAPTER 9

DOWN UNDER

I WAS EXCITED when Ford England asked me to take part in the London to Sydney Marathon Rally. I knew it was going to be a huge undertaking, although I wasn't exactly sure what it would entail, but I said yes straight away. It was all the more exciting because I was going to represent Ireland and drive a Cortina Lotus that was assembled in Cork. I have fond memories of that car; the registration number was VPI 77 and it was cream with lime green stripes.

The London to Sydney Marathon ran from 24 November to 18 December 1968, with 243 men and 12 women entering the 10,000-mile competition. There were 98 cars with crews from 19 nations, some professional drivers in factory-backed cars and some private individuals. The idea originated when Sir Max Aitken, proprietor of the *Daily Express*, and two of his editorial executives came up with the idea over a business lunch in late 1967. The *Daily Express* put up a first prize of £10,000 ($24,000) and the

Australian Sydney Telegraph awarded runner-up cash prizes. The *Daily Express* in London and the *Australian Sydney Telegraph* promoted the event, saying it was to be a spectacular feat of driving and human endurance. And they were right: this unique motorsport event captured the hearts and minds of millions of people all over the world, and I was part of it.

The route was carefully mapped out and the border controls organised by an eight-man team headed by Tommy Sopwith, a British businessman and former racing driver, and Jack Sears, popularly known as 'Gentleman Jack', who was a well-known figure in rallying. The route covered 7,000 miles, through 11 countries in as many days, before reaching the Australian outback and continuing a further 3,000 miles. I thought the Circuit of Ireland and the Monte Carlo Rally were big events but this was something else.

The only drawback was that I would have preferred to choose my co-driver/navigator. On any long trip you need to have someone you have confidence in, someone who knows your little foibles and who will be good company. Henry Taylor, Ford's competition manager at that time, decided that Lucette Pointet should drive with me. She was an accomplished French rally driver and navigator who usually worked for Citroën, but there were communication problems from the start. I had never driven with Lucette before and I wasn't going to let this opportunity pass me by just because I couldn't choose my own navigator. Before we left, there was a big launch in Jurys Hotel in Dublin and we had smart white wool suits made for us by the British Wool Marketing Board. The whole outfit was totally impractical but it was just for publicity purposes. All the Ford team wore the same outfits.

Ford decided that the team should go to Gamecock Barracks, an army training camp in Yorkshire, to make sure we were in good physical health for the marathon rally. They were right to do this, of course, because it was obvious that the rally would make great physical and mental demands on us. I didn't see it like that at the time and thought I was in top form and ready for everything. The men in charge put us through an army fitness course, where we had to jog, run, lift weights and do press-ups each morning and generally push ourselves to the limit of our endurance. I wasn't very happy with all that, but I did it anyway and there were compensations. The army officers involved in the training were very friendly and put us through our paces with great enthusiasm, as well as providing good company and entertainment in the evening.

Detailed instructions were given on how to get out of the car if it should go into a lake, information I am glad to say that I never had to use. The serious part was having the route outlined to us: ferry from Dover to Calais, on to Paris and then into Italy, Yugoslavia, Bulgaria, Turkey, across the Bosphorus and then into Iran, Afghanistan, Pakistan, and finally, arriving in Bombay. I think it was only then that I realised this wasn't going to be all fun and games, but I was up for it whatever happened.

We started from Crystal Palace Stadium in South London and my mum and dad and Aunt Lily came over to see me off. There were originally meant to be 100 cars in the rally, but in the end only 98 set off. We were car number 93 and so had to wait until 92 other cars were flagged away before we could take to the road. Eighty thousand people saw us leave the stadium and millions more lined the streets all the way to Dover, where the *Maid of Kent* was waiting to take us to Calais. During the crossing we were advised that we should not take the main road through Paris, as previously planned, because there would be no police escort. This was no handicap to me as I had plenty of experience driving through France, and in any case, didn't I have a Frenchwoman sitting beside me?

Lucette and I should never have been teamed up. She was gentle and softly spoken, while I was my usual self, and driven. Her English wasn't great, not that she spoke much; she just sat reading the road book and occasionally looked up to tell me to turn right or whatever. I don't think she liked me any more than I did her. She did very little of the driving because it was a right-hand drive car, which she didn't like. Some of the roads we went over were right-hand and some left-hand roads, which made it tricky at times.

Lucette was not enjoying the rally and she was either *très fatigué* or she wanted to *manger*. When we arrived in Milan, her mother, a very pleasant woman, was there to meet us with a bag containing a small knife and a huge garlic sausage for Lucette. I swear it was about 18 inches long and as thick as a milk bottle. As we drove through Italy, Yugoslavia and into Bulgaria, every time Lucette opened that bag to slice a piece of the sausage the smell was unbearable. I think we were somewhere in Turkey when I grabbed her sausage and threw it out of the window. I know it was unkind of me but I couldn't stand it any more. In any case, it was the sausage ended any chance of an *entente cordiale*!

Up until Istanbul everything had been going fine, apart from the icy silence from the seat beside me, but after that things changed. We crossed the Bosphorus at dawn and it was just as if we had left one world and entered another. In reality, we had merely left Europe for Asia, but to me it was like leaving civilisation behind. The lorry drivers drove like madmen in Turkey and that drive to Sivas had to be taken at a slow pace to avoid a collision. It seemed as if everyone had come out to greet us and there were hundreds of men thronging the streets, with police trying to hold them back.

Ahead of us lay the 176 miles of unsurfaced mountain roads to Erzinican, the first really difficult part of the rally, and it was raining. The winding roads and wooden bridges made the going challenging, but finally there was a down-hill straight run to Erzinican and a brief rest. The road to Tehran was generally good, but arriving there was a night-mare as the traffic was horrendous and little Vespa taxis sprang out from nowhere.

We had covered 3,600 miles in four days and passed through three time zones but still we were only halfway to Bombay. We drove on through the Iranian/Afghani border without any trouble and were now headed for Kabul. As we drove through the desert, the car was not running well; we were going slower and slower until finally the pistons packed up completely. As I may have already mentioned, I know very little about the workings of motor cars, I just like driving them, especially when they are in good working order. We had come to an abrupt stop in the middle of Afghanistan in the desert, and the heat was appalling. Lucette was muttering away in French but there was nothing I could do about it, the car just wouldn't go.

As we sat there, hoping that one of the other cars would arrive to help us, camels and their riders appeared out of the sand dunes with the sun glaring behind them. Lucette became agitated, and I didn't blame her, because the men, all dressed in white robes and turbans, advanced menacingly towards us, looking as if they had just come off the set of *Lawrence of Arabia*. The man who appeared to be the leader of the tribe climbed down from his camel and approached, waving his hand for me to get out of the car. I stood there in front of him, and when he spoke I feared the heat had got to me because his English was perfect and he sounded as if he had been educated in Cambridge. I tried to explain the situation and he listened patiently, but his comrades were not so civilised as their English-speaking leader. They began pointing to the boot of the car. I opened it, but all it contained were some small cans of oil, which they must have thought were Coca-Cola or something because one of them whipped off the top and began drinking it before spitting it out in disgust.

Lucette by this time was crouched in the car in tears. The men were pulling at my watch and bracelet and touching my blonde hair, which was no doubt a novelty to them. I smiled and tried to remain calm, all the while thinking that this wasn't going to end well, when out of nowhere I heard a car approaching. I can still recall the relief of seeing that car racing along the road towards us. The Ford Cortina was driven by two British army officers, Lieutenant Martin Proudlock and Captain David Harrison, and, unlike ours, this car had all four pistons running. When I turned to look, I was amazed to see the camels and men had vanished as quickly as they had appeared. I met David at an event recently and I asked him, did he fire a gun to frighten the men away, but he said he had no gun; they must have seen the car in the distance and decided to leave. I might have thought I had been hallucinating, if it wasn't for the camel droppings all around and Lucette whimpering.

Martin and David said they would tow us; they could hardly leave us all alone in the desert, but they knew it would slow them down. It was beginning to get dark as the tow rope was attached to our car and the temperature was dropping rapidly. It was freezing in the car because no engine meant no heating and so we swapped seats as we went along so that no one would have to endure long stretches in the cold. To add to our troubles, the rope snapped several times and got shorter and shorter as it was retied. The men remained calm and never seemed to lose their patience although they were probably raging inside. Towing could put you out of the competition, but we took a chance and trundled on. I knew we might be out of the event at this stage, but luck and Stuart Turner were on my side.

We got into Kabul hours late, at about 3 a.m. At the checkpoint, Stuart Turner, a gorgeous man who I was absolutely mad about, waved us in and stamped our time card. He was competition manager for the British Motor Corporation (BMC) and the stage end official. I met him recently at a dinner and when I told him that I had always wanted to drive for him, he said, 'Why didn't you ask?' But I would never have had the courage to do that as a young woman. After all, he was at that time one of the most influential and accomplished managers in the business.

As we were so late, the hotel had let out our room to Afghan tribesmen, who were in the city for a cattle fair the next day. The room was meant for two people but there were about 10 of them sleeping there and the smell was dreadful. We decided to sleep in the lobby, where the fleas hopped around us for the rest of the night.

The company plane had flown in to Kabul with journalists, champagne and caviar, but no pistons. We had some makeshift repairs done in Kabul, but because the pistons had failed to arrive we were still struggling. We opted to take an alternative route from Kabul to Sarobi to avoid the Lataband Pass, but this was not allowed – we could have been disqualified as we were approaching from the wrong direction. Instead, we turned back and the only thing to do was to carry on to the border crossing at Torkham, which meant we had ahead of us the Khyber Pass, connecting Afghanistan and Pakistan.

Lucette was insisting we give up, but I refused. I knew as well as she did that the damaged pistons might not survive the steep inclines of the Khyber Pass, so I took my father's advice from long ago: 'If a car won't go forward, it'll go in reverse.' So that's exactly what I did. I turned the car around and drove the 33 miles of steep, winding roads in reverse. Rod Waller, the Australian cartoonist I mentioned before, sent me the most wonderful cartoon illustrating that drive over the Khyber Pass. He must be a fan of mine!

Once through the Pass, we descended towards Peshawar, where there were crowds of onlookers pushing themselves forward as well as chaotic traffic. Young boys were throwing rocks or trying to grab windscreen wipers as we drove to the Indian border. The border crossing was handled well despite the tensions between the two countries. Both the Indian and the Pakistani officials were so enthusiastic about the rally that they put their differences aside and the crossing only took a matter of minutes.

Safely into India, we set off on the 280-mile run to New Delhi. The road before us was a narrow strip of tarmac. Livestock, ox carts, bicycles and thousands of people

appeared at every village. They were friendly, but it was very hard to avoid running into them as they leapt out into the road, waving and shouting in their hysterical excitement. As we approached Indore, we were reduced to a crawling speed to avoid running into the crowd.

The Cortina Lotus chugged into Bombay on 2 December, still with only three pistons, and I was happy and relieved that we had made it. We checked in and the car was immediately put into *parc fermé*. This literally means 'closed park' and is the secure area where the cars went for repair. Tired and exhausted, and as much in need of a rest as the car was, we made our way to the hotel that Ford had booked for us. The hotel manager took one look at us and said we couldn't possibly stay there. 'It's not safe for women,' he said. 'You must go to the Sun-n-Sand Hotel.'

This was a hotel on the beach and I later learned that it is where crews from the airlines stayed on their stopovers. I didn't know if Ford was going to be happy to pay for that, but the manager of the hotel insisted we couldn't stay there. He wouldn't even let us go out into the street to get a taxi and made us wait inside until he found a driver who he decided would deliver us safely to the hotel.

The Sun-n-Sand Hotel was luxurious and we stayed there for a few days awaiting our fate and attending cocktail parties in downtown Bombay. I was concerned because we were the 72nd car and there were only supposed to be 70 cars allowed on to the liner to ferry us to Fremantle. But I needn't have worried because Stuart Turner made sure we got on to the SS *Chusan*: he knew how hard I had worked to get there and he wasn't going to leave me behind. Before we left Bombay the cars were drained of petrol, steam cleaned and then loaded into the hold of the 24,000-ton ocean liner, by crane. The next time I would see the Cortina was in Fremantle, Australia. It was one of the last runs for that P&O liner, and it showed. It was a nine-day voyage with one stop at Colombo on the island of Ceylon, or Sri Lanka as it is now.

By the time we got on that ship on 4 December my relationship with Lucette hadn't improved and we were hardly speaking. I put my bag in my cabin and went into the bar with the boys, who I knew well, having been rallying and racing with most of them in the past. We were having a great time but I was worried about Lucette, who had disappeared. Bad as our relationship was, I didn't want to ignore her altogether, so I went to find her.

The cabin I had been assigned was a First Class one, and when I arrived my case was sitting outside the door. I knocked a few times and all I heard was Lucette shouting, '*Allez-vous-en!*' My French is not good, but I knew this meant 'Go away'. I did go away, to find the purser, and he confirmed that the cabin was mine; he came down with me to rectify the situation. Lucette was in the cabin with her boyfriend, who was driving for the Citroën team, and she told me I could use his cabin down in the bowels of the ship. Furious, I told her it was my drive, my sponsorship, and that they should leave. I never saw either of them for the rest of the voyage; it's easy to avoid people on a big liner like the SS *Chusan*.

When we anchored in the harbour at Colombo, a flotilla of boats came to greet us and members of the local motoring club showed us the sights. That night, a dinner was served in the Mount Lavinia Hotel overlooking the ocean and a dancing display was organised, especially for us. The warmth of our reception and the hospitality shown were amazing. It was a pleasant interlude before the boredom that would set in on the rest of the journey.

As we entered the Bay of Bengal, the sea was rough and choppy. It was so bad that the water in the swimming pool on the top deck splashed over the side, saturating a man from one of the big London newspapers as he sat typing; the pool was drained after that. There was so much turbulence that a lot of the crews were sick and confined to their cabins. We were nine days on the ship and the PR people weren't happy when Paddy Hopkirk told a BBC television crew that the sea journey was the best advertisement for air travel he could imagine.

We arrived in Fremantle on 13 December and spent our time checking maps and making sure the car was ready for the next stage of the marathon. From there, we drove 20 miles in convoy to Perth, escorted by the police, with a stern warning about Australian speed limits. We arrived at Gloucester Park horse race track at 11 p.m. and there were no spectators to watch us do a lap of honour: horses, their owners and spectators were long gone. The next morning, spectators did turn up to see the cars lined up around the race track and watch them leave at three-minute intervals. We had three days to complete the 3,000 miles to Sydney and the Cortina was running on two cylinders. There were no proper roads, just bush country, with the possibility of kangaroos jumping out at you. We had a kangaroo bar on the front of the car but if one of those hit us, roo bar or not, we could be off the road.

After leaving Perth we travelled 340 miles to Youanmi, once a gold mining town, but now there was nothing but a signpost, which we could barely see through the dust. On then for a further 200-odd miles to Marvel Loch, another mining town but this time with a few inhabitants and houses, before reaching Lake King. Ahead of us were 900 miles of outback across the Nullabor Plain, with unpaved roads, barely visible tracks and more bull dust. It was a treeless wilderness and difficult to see where the road began and the bush ended. The Cortina was trudging along but getting there, despite the fact that now, as well as the pistons, we had suspension problems.

On the way from Mingary to Menindee, we arrived at a place appropriately named Broken Hill, an isolated mining town. It wasn't a hill so much as a mound, but we were stuck and couldn't move. Some of the other cars were going so fast that they were able to fly over, but we couldn't get up speed and needed a push. There were plenty of people around willing to help us, but RAC Steward Jack Kemsley was looking after this stage. 'Please, Jack,' I said, 'just let them push me over the hill.' 'No, no, you'll have to wait until all the cars come through. It's too dangerous,' was his response.

I was livid. Some cars had broken down along the way, we had made up quite a bit of time despite our mechanical problems and we were in with a chance of the Coupe des Dames, but Jack would not budge. Eventually we got going again, and with the wilderness behind us and a flat road ahead I was feeling confident we could finish in time.

Dawn on the last day was breaking as we drove into the Australian Alps and crossed the mountain ranges from Edi up and over Mount Buffalo to Brookside and around Mount Feathertop across Snowy Mountains to Numeralla in New South Wales. The long winding mountain roads with extremely deep inclines were a nightmare and my arms were aching with all the gear changes I had to make to get us through them. It was only 36 miles from Numeralla to the next stage at Hindmarsh Station, but just 14 miles of that was asphalt and the rest very rough gravel. The end was in sight and I was exhausted. We were back on a tarmac road and Warwick Farm was only 80 miles away. I was aware that dire warnings had been issued by the NSW police about speed limits being infringed but I just put my foot down and disregarded all the signs; it was my only hope.

The inevitable happened. I heard a siren, saw flashing lights and a police car pulled up in front of us. The policeman put on his hat and walked menacingly towards our car. I couldn't help it, I broke down and the tears were running down my face – after all my hard work, this was going to be the end. The police officer approached the car and looked at me. 'Are you the Irish girl?' he said. I could only nod my head. 'You've had a lot of trouble, haven't you?' I sniffed my agreement. There had been a lot of coverage of the event on the Australian media and that policeman had obviously been watching my progress. 'My grandmother was from Cork.' Thank God for those Irish ancestors, I thought. 'Don't you worry, put on your hazard lights and just follow me.' 'I might not be able to stay with you if you go up a hill,' I replied. 'It's OK, it's on the flat to Warwick Farm. I'm out of my district, but I won't let you down.'

He put the lights on the top of his car and with the siren blaring we followed, dodging in and out and keeping close to our police escort. He brought us the 30 miles to Warwick Farm and left us there, and I was so sorry I didn't ever get a chance to say goodbye and thank him. We were so late that the first cars had gone and most of the press too. Fifty-six of the 98 cars finished and we were 48th; only for those pistons and Jack Kemsley, we would have done much better but it was an achievement to finish at all. I left the car in the car park underneath the hotel for the Ford managers to take care of. The Cortina Lotus, VPI 77, is still alive and living in England somewhere. I never saw Lucette leave; she didn't even say goodbye, she just seemed to disappear.

I boarded the plane in Sydney bound for London, from where I would fly home to Dublin. Not long after take-off, one of the Ford administrators handed me a bundle of telegrams and letters. Why he had to wait until we were on the plane to do that, I'll never know. I was overwhelmed as I sat there reading them, knowing that we very nearly didn't make it. After suffering the Afghan tribesmen in the desert, fleas in Kabul, faulty pistons, turbulent seas, Mademoiselle Lucette and dusty excuses for roads, the telegrams and letters of congratulations were a godsend. One of the letters was from Joe Hardy, who was the owner of Searsons Bar in Upper Baggot Street, Dublin, telling me that he was throwing a party for me on 21 December. What a wonderful evening that was! I was surrounded by family, friends and well-wishers and champagne corks were popping all night. That party was the best ending I could have wished for after the 230 hours of driving from London to Sydney.

The London to Sydney had been the greatest driving event of my life so far and I wondered if my next big adventure could possibly surpass it. I didn't know what to expect when I undertook the longest rally ever to take place – the 1970 Daily Mirror World Cup Rally from London to Mexico.

CHAPTER 10

SOUTH OF THE BORDER

THE LONDON TO Sydney Marathon was a success in as much as I finished, when 42 other competitors had fallen by the wayside. It was well known in the industry that I had overcome many obstacles along the way on that rally and no doubt it was because of this that British Leyland got the notion that I was a good bet for the mammoth 1970 World Cup London to Mexico Rally. The sun was shining when Sir Alf Ramsey and Bobby Moore, captain of the England team, were at the Wembley Stadium, waving a Union Jack to see everyone on their way. As we posed for photographs, Lord Stokes, head of British Leyland, said to us, 'Girls, if you get as far as Dover, I will be very happy.' It was just as if he was patting a little girl on the head with this patronising remark.

Yet again I was being used for publicity purposes – British Leyland needed all the exposure it could manage because the Austin Maxi was a new car on the market. I don't think they really cared if I got there or not, as long as

I flashed my legs and looked pretty. We posed before the orange and white candy striped Austin in full-length white coats and white leather boots. The outfits were amazing but totally impractical for rallying. Our rally outfits were a blue jacket and red trousers. Alice Watson and Ginette de Rolland were my co-drivers, and before we left we had inoculations for yellow fever, typhoid, cholera and smallpox.

The British Leyland team had done everything they could to make the car, which was a new and untried model, ready for the long trip. A huge rubber bag fuel tank was installed and other modifications made. Nobody could know how the Maxi would respond to the long drive or whether it would get beyond Lisbon.

The *Daily Mirror* was quick to take up sponsorship when approached by Paddy Hopkirk and Wylton Dickson, an expatriate Australian and one of the promoters of the London to Sydney. The story goes that Paddy and Wylton were at a drinks party and dreamt up the idea of a rally from Wembley to the Estadio Azteca, Mexico City, visiting the capitals of all the countries that played in the 1966 FIFA World Cup. The *Daily Mirror* was one of Britain's largest daily newspapers and their readers were avid football fans. The *Daily Express* had achieved great success from the London to Sydney sponsorship so the proprietors of the *Daily Mirror* immediately saw the potential of combining both football and motorsport. England had won the World Cup in 1966 at Wembley and the next final was to be held in Mexico in 1970. It was fantastic publicity for cars to drive through football-mad South America just before the beginning of the 1970 FIFA World Cup to be held in the Estadio Aztec, especially with Jimmy Greaves as one of the competitors. Jimmy had recently retired from international football after a very successful career with England. The *Daily Mirror* stumped up £250,000 (£3.7 million today) to stage the event. Dean Dalamount of the RAC was consulted and he asked rally legend John Sprinzel to plan the route.

Alice, Ginette and I climbed into our orange and white striped Austin Maxi on 19 April 1970, knowing that the epic drive to Mexico would end on 22 May, if we managed to get that far. Our Maxi was 1475cc, which was much smaller than the rest of the team, who had cars with 1800cc

engines. British Leyland had assembled celebrated company for the trip. The other Austin Maxis were driven by the Red Arrows, the Royal Air Force Aerobatic Team and HRH Prince Michael of Kent, then a young army officer, with the Royal Hussars team. On the long drive, Alice and I would have imaginary conversations about being asked to tea at the palace: 'Cucumber sandwiches, anybody?' – anything to keep us awake.

Ninety-eight cars, from 22 countries, started out from Wembley. There were Minis and Fords from Britain, Moskviches from Russia, a Toyota from Japan, a Beach Buggy, a Wagoneer Jeep from the US and even two Rolls-Royces. The course covered over 16,000 miles (25,700 km), 5,000 miles through Europe and the rest through South and Central America. The London to Sydney was a marathon, but nothing compared to this.

I was carried away by the preparations for this enormous undertaking and completely oblivious to everything else. Momentous events were occurring which went completely over my head. In Ireland, the Arms Crisis was just erupting. Charles Haughey, Minister for Finance, and Neil Blaney, Minister for Agriculture and Fisheries, had been asked to resign by Jack Lynch, the Taoiseach. They were accused of the attempted illegal importation of arms for use by the Provisional IRA. The Troubles in Northern Ireland were escalating at a fierce rate. Meanwhile, the UK was on the brink of a general election, which would see the Conservative Edward Heath win a surprise victory over

Labour Prime Minister Harold Wilson. But all these political disturbances meant nothing to me. My mind was focused on the project in hand and nothing was going to stop me doing my very best to get to Mexico in one piece.

The drive through Europe was not difficult, although the dust and roads in Yugoslavia were challenging, but 5,000 miles is a long way on any continent. During the seven days of the European leg there was only one scheduled overnight stop – in Monza, Italy – and we took it in turns to sleep. By the time we reached Lisbon, only 71 cars were left out of the 96 starters. Our Austin Maxi was loaded on to the SS *Derwent*, bound for a 12-day journey to Rio de Janeiro, across the South Atlantic, along with the rest of the remaining cars. The SS *Derwent* was a freight ship that didn't take passengers so we had to fly from Lisbon Airport to Rio in a Boeing 707 to await the arrival of our car. We stayed in the Hotel Gloria, the rally headquarters in Rio de Janeiro, and this was a welcome rest before the next leg. The media were all over us when we got there. As I stepped into the hotel swimming pool in my white bikini the flash-bulbs were popping. No doubt that's what British Leyland was hoping for, and I didn't let them down!

Alice, Ginette and I made good use of our time in Rio. We visited the beauty salons to get our nails and hair done, we went shopping and did the usual touristy things, which, of course, included a visit to the Christ the Redeemer Monument on Mount Corcovado. The beaches were beautiful and the famous Copacabana, two and a half miles of sand with the mountains in the background, was a delight. Terry Kingsley, one of the Red Arrow team, went down to the beach at Ipanema to go for a swim, and even though he thought he had carefully hidden his wallet it was gone when he came in from the water.

Paddy Hopkirk and some of the others flew out to Costa Rica and further afield to make recces but we just lay back and relaxed. One evening, Alan Zafer, who was the PR person for British Leyland, said we had all been invited to the British Embassy for a reception. We arrived at the beautiful, ranch-style house and were graciously received. After a few drinks, I asked, was the Ambassador at home and could I meet him? I was brought over to this man, who clicked his heels together and kissed my hand. I knew immediately something was not quite right. By mistake, we had gone to the Russian Embassy! We finished our drinks and left discreetly.

The Red Arrows team were good company and took great care of us. The evening before we left to start the drive to Mexico, we all went to the cinema to see a film that was just out: *Butch Cassidy and the Sundance Kid*. Next day, like Paul Newman, I was back in the saddle and the fun and games were over for the time being; the real work was about to begin. On Friday, 8 May, we departed from outside the São Paulo Museum of Art in Rio de Janeiro to a flag-waving crowd, loud music and excited pressmen at the start of our journey through Brazil. BMC's competition manager Stuart Turner was concerned about the floods forecast, and when the rain came we had to contend with hailstones the size of golf balls crashing down on us. Some of the drivers pulled over and took shelter under the trees but I saw no need for that and just kept going. Crossing the narrow wooden bridges, which appeared out of nowhere, was challenging. There was no other way round, so although they looked precarious we just had to keep going. No road signs were to be seen on the route to Uruguay, and at one point, where a road diverged, we had to stop and ask the way.

After 40 hours of non-stop driving we reached Montevideo on Sunday 10 May. We were one of only 52 cars that had got that far. After a much-needed night's sleep, we boarded the ferry, along with our cars, for the three-hour journey across the River Plate to Buenos Aires. The cars were unloaded, and once through the crazy city traffic we set off through Argentina for Saladillo, our next time control, a journey of 125 miles. The tracks were dry, quite smooth but very dusty, and we made good time.

We arrived in Chile for an overnight in Santiago, where we slept but not for long because on Thursday, 14 May, we were up again at 5 a.m. to begin another 57 hours of driving. The drive from Santiago to La Paz in Bolivia was over the Andes, through tracks of extremely high altitude. Oxygen had been provided for everyone but we never used it. Some of the men got altitude sickness but it never seemed to affect us. We were climbing over 15,000 feet and the roads were made of loose, very dusty gravel. They were mostly tracks and when you did get on a proper road you wondered where the noise had gone. It was hard, but if the car kept going, so would I – I am always determined to finish! I drove a lot of the time. It wasn't that I didn't trust Ginette or Alice, but if anyone was going to put us off the road I preferred it to be me.

Ginette and Alice didn't always hit it off. Alice would make some smart remark to Ginette and she would respond with a cutting reply. I was never sure about the pecking order between them. As far as I was concerned, they were both very capable women and I was happy to have them on my team.

We drove through the amazing landscape of Central America with barely time to register what was around us, although with my dress-designing hat on I couldn't miss the women. Their clothes were like nothing I had ever seen before. Everywhere in the mountains you would see them in beautiful garments of vibrant red, orange, blue and green, and they always wore hats – wonderful, wide-brimmed hats. I had thoughts of importing those colourful outfits into Dublin, but it never happened. Like many of my bright ideas, it came to nothing.

With the words of British Leyland's Lord Stokes still lingering in my mind, I couldn't waste too much time admiring the natives or gazing at the landscape. Although we had come further than Dover, there were still many miles ahead of us and I wanted to show him how wrong he was. He obviously didn't have much faith in his female team or in the Austin Maxi we were driving, but it never gave me much trouble. There were only two things that went wrong with that car: the cassette player and the fan belt. On a very bumpy road, the cassette player started of its own accord and suddenly Elvis was singing 'All Shook Up'. I nearly jumped out of my skin; Alice managed to turn him off before I got too excited. But that was only a minor thing; the fan belt was a little more serious. Fan belts went quite often in cars in those days, and when I saw the temperature gauge going up and up I knew we were in trouble. We stopped at the top of the mountain and waited for someone to come along. As luck would have it, Tony Fall, who was driving a Ford Escort, came to our rescue. Jimmy Greaves was his co-driver and was really only there for publicity purposes, but as it turned out he was a very good driver as well as a footballer. His footballing days were nearly over, but his popularity remained – he was a charming man.

That wasn't the first time that the fan belt snapped. It went on the first leg in Portugal and I didn't have a spare to hand so I used my tights. It was headlines in the British newspapers: 'Rosemary takes her tights off' – more publicity for Lord Stokes. Tony Fall put the fan belt on and we were ready to go. We looked around for Alice, but she was nowhere to be seen. When we found her, she looked like a little green shrub as she was covered in cactus flies bigger than grasshoppers and they were sucking her arms, face and any bit of skin that was exposed. We tried to hit them off, but they must have liked her Scottish blood and wouldn't move. The only thing I could think of was to take the fire extinguisher and spray her all over. I was told afterwards they could have given her awful burns, but it worked. The horrible insects fell off and we got her into the car and drove off.

As the day wore on, Alice blew up like a balloon and was covered in what looked like a very bad case of measles. When we got to the control stop, I had to cut off her clothes, her watch and everything. We fed her glucose drinks just to keep her going. When we arrived at La Paz I knew we had to get her to hospital because she was drifting in and out of consciousness. The stewards at the top of the mountain were insisting that I couldn't go down as it was past 12 midnight. It was a very narrow pass, with cliffs on one side and a deep drop on the other. We were told that trucks were due to be coming up throughout the night. I crashed through a barrier that the stewards had put across the road; I was sure Alice would die if we didn't get help for her. Halfway down the pass, we could see trucks approaching and Ginette put her foot on the horn and kept it there. Someone must have telephoned and said some mad women are coming down the mountain, keep out of their way. I didn't care if the car was damaged, I just wanted to get Alice to the hospital. There was an ambulance in *parc ferme* waiting for us and we handed Alice over.

We had an overnight in La Paz, and when Ginette and I went back to the hotel we resigned ourselves to the fact that this was the end for us and the rally. If you started with a team of three, all of you had to finish – that was the rule. Later the next day there was a knock on the door and there she was, with her feet barely touching the ground, as two male nurses held her up. Alice knew if she didn't come with us we were out of the running and she wouldn't have that. She was a tiny little thing with a strong Scottish accent and she could drink a bottle of whisky and be up again the next morning, not a bother. Ginette and Alice were the best of friends after that episode.

Alice still wasn't well, but at least we had medication for her and an assurance from the doctor that she would recover. And so we left La Paz on Sunday, 17 May, en route to Lima in Peru to cover another 1,150 miles in the target time of 25 hours. We strapped Alice into the back of the car and hoped for the best. The going was rough – nine of the 39 cars that left La Paz never made it to Lima. At this stage, apart from us, there were two other female crews still in the running: Claudine Trautmann in a Citroën and Jean Denton in an Austin 1800.

We left Lima from the Automobile Club of Peru on Tuesday evening, 19 May, after a sleep that didn't feel long enough. The jungle-lined tracks to the Ecuadorian border in Macará kept us awake as we bumped along. It was a relief to cross the border and begin the journey to Saraguro on the smooth dirt roads. We crossed the border into Colombia and the drive from Cali to Buenaventura was all twisting narrow roads, mainly through jungle. There were trucks and overcrowded buses everywhere and the slip-streams of dust that came after them nearly choked us. The only consolation was that it was mostly downhill as we were approaching the coast. At this stage we were looking forward to the luxury of sailing up the Panama Canal and getting a good night's sleep.

Twenty-six cars got as far as the port at Buenaventura to board the MS *Verdi* for the two-day trip to Central America. MS *Verdi* was a beautiful ship, with a swimming pool and well-appointed cabins. It was pure luxury after the over-night stop in Buenaventura, where the hotel was disgusting, with one antiquated refrigerator covered in insects. When we got on the ship, the first thing I did was to put on my now infamous white bikini and jump in the pool with some of the boys. In the evening, the captain decided we were going to have a fancy-dress party and we all got dressed up and danced into the night. The sensible ones went to bed because we still had miles to go – there were six more coun-tries to drive through before we reached Mexico City.

The voyage took two and a half days. We sailed up the Pacific coast of Colombia and then through the Panama Canal on 23 May. The ship docked for the night in Cristóbal, and although we enjoyed the diversion we were all anxious to get on with it. Alice was doing well, and after the rest on the boat she was almost back to her old self. We had to wait overnight for the cars to be unloaded and on the following day the cars were released from the *parc fermé*.

The 350 miles from Panama City to San José in Costa Rica were on tarmacked roads and easier than anything we had driven on since we left Lisbon. Once we reached Costa Rica, however, we were in coffee plantation territory and into a mountainous region, where the roads changed from tarmac to dirt tracks and we were driving in the dark. We did well on that leg and all we had to do now was get through Nicaragua, Honduras, El Salvador and Guatemala, on what turned out to be fairly good roads, before finally reaching Mexico.

At the border between Costa Rica and Nicaragua the national cleansing department sprayed all the cars with disinfectant. We were well and truly fumigated and the smell in the car was awful as we drove off, full of confidence that we would get to Mexico City in one piece. It was in the early hours of the morning and dark except for our headlights glaring when we came round a bend to find huge rocks blocking our way across the track. Half-joking, of course, I said to Alice and Ginette, 'You had better get out and move them out of the way.' That's when we heard the sound of horses' hooves and five men on horseback galloped towards us with big sombreros and handkerchiefs tied around their faces. When they realised we were women, they started to question us. 'What are you doing?' We explained we were on a rally. 'Where are you going?' Mexico City, we told them. 'What have you got in the car?' We told them nothing but a few clothes. Then they proceeded to lecture us, telling us that we shouldn't be out in the middle of the night, how very dangerous it was and cautioned us to be careful. They acted like true gentlemen, rolled the rocks out of the way and left us to it.

We went on and the long hours of driving were starting to take their toll on me. 'How much longer, Alice?' I asked. 'How much longer?' 'Not too long now,' she said, trying to encourage me to keep going. 'Soon, soon,' she added, looking at the road book, and just then we came over the brow of the hill and all the lights were spread out below us. It was Fortín, a night halt 300 miles from Mexico City, and we had made it to the last checkpoint.

The day before we made our entrance to the Estadio Azteca we stayed in a beautiful hotel in Fortín. The owner was an Englishman who ran a sugar plantation, and he and the rest of the staff there made a great fuss of us. The magnificent swimming pool was covered in gardenias and there were flowers everywhere. But, somehow, it was a bit of an anticlimax after all those days of hard driving. I found it hard to relax and take in that we had actually made it to the finish. There were 98 contestants in all and only 23 arrived at the Estadio Azteca in Mexico. Five female crews left Wembley that day, two made it to the finish and we were one of them, gaining 10th place overall and beating 11 other all-male teams. The Red Arrows team came 22nd and Prince Michael of Kent went off the road 10 miles from Rio and withdrew. Tony Fall and Jimmy Greaves made it to 6th place.

The cars were washed and polished and we had a police escort into the stadium. Suddenly, the rain came down in torrents and all the spectators, who might have enjoyed the spectacle of 23 cars, in various states of disrepair, speeding along, disappeared. As we approached the Estadio Azteca the rain eased off and the cars got in line. The first three headed by Hannu Mikkola and Gunnar Palm, the winners, were to enter first, and because we had won the Ladies' Section we were to go in after them. I was fuming when Jean Denton, driving a BMC 1800, otherwise known as a 'land crab', who had come 18th, nipped in front and drove into the stadium before me.

A telegram from Alec Issigonis, designer of the Maxi, congratulating us on winning the Ladies' Prize

Jean was a Yorkshirewoman and later became Baroness Denton of Wakefield. She was a very clever and talented woman and I got on well with her, but at that moment I hated her. I didn't hold a grudge, I rarely do that, and when Jean became a Minister in Stormont she invited me to Northern Ireland on several occasions and we had good times together. Sadly, she has since died.

It was pure determination that we finished that rally – well, that and my outstanding driving skills, of course! But there were things that happened on the event that really annoyed me. There was another women's team and we passed them broken down on the side of the road. When we offered help, they waved us on. '*Finito*,' they said, indicating that it was all over for them. When we got to the next control, there they were, driving in. In any case, it didn't matter, because in the end they didn't finish. We won £1,000 and shared it between us. That was a lot of money and the equivalent today would be over £14,000. We all went into Mexico City and bought stunning white lace dresses. I had mine for years after: it had a round neck and an A-line skirt, well above the knees. I also bought a beautiful ruby and diamond ring, which unfortunately, was stolen years later from my home, along with an emerald ring I owned.

The next month, June 1970, Alice and I drove together in the Scottish Rally, in another Austin Maxi. We had spent so much time together and were now great friends. I was to get married in August, and although I hadn't planned to have a bridesmaid I decided to ask Alice and she accepted. She and her husband, Andy, came over from Scotland for the wedding and I was glad to have them by my side. On the day of the wedding, Andy drove me to the church. I was very quiet in the car and he knew something was wrong. 'You don't really want to do this, do you, Rosie?' he said to me. 'Stay in the car and we'll just drive off somewhere. You can telephone and say you've changed your mind.'

How I wish I had taken him up on his offer. He was right: I didn't want to get married, I didn't want to be any man's property, and in 1970s Ireland when you were married you belonged to your husband. I knew in my heart that it wouldn't work and I should never have gone through with it, silly me!

CHAPTER 11

MEN, MARRIAGE AND MORTGAGES

I WAS ENGAGED to be married several times, but when I had to choose between the man and the motor the car always won. They all wrongly assumed that I would give up motorsports when I married and I had to tell them that this was not the case. A lot of the time I said yes to a proposal to prove to myself, and my mother, that I could get a man, but really I had no intention of settling down.

I was very young and dress designing when one of my brother's friends brought his fiancée into our showroom. I made a few dresses for her, and when they were ready they would come in together to collect them. One day, he came in to collect a dress and asked me to go for a coffee with him and he told me it was all off with his fiancée. After that we started to go out now and again, but as far as I was concerned he was just a friend. To tell the truth, the thing that attracted me was his Triumph TR2 sports car, which he let me drive! I was driving down the old Belfast Road, near St Margaret's on the way to Drogheda, when we came to a very sharp right-hand bend and at the speed I was going there was no way I was going to make it. I spun round and round in the middle of the road, luckily hitting nothing, and ended up facing the way we had just come. He didn't say a word; I could do no wrong as far as he was concerned.

He got it into his head that we should get married and I was noncommittal and humoured him until one day I came home to find a strange woman sitting in the drawing room with my mother. The woman smiled when she saw me and said that she had flown in from Mexico because she had to bring the veil for the wedding. She said it was a family heirloom, which couldn't possibly be trusted to the post, so she had brought it personally. 'Who is the veil for?' I asked, bewildered. 'Well, you, of course,' she replied, 'when you marry my nephew. It's a family tradition and he told me you were getting married very soon.' I told her she had made a mistake, and walked out. Apparently she stayed for ages, trying to persuade my mother that I should marry her nephew. She was going to leave him a lot of money and she would love it if he married me.

I didn't see him again until years later, when I went to do the RAC Rally in England. He was in the hotel at Heathrow standing behind a huge potted plant in the foyer with a crash helmet on and driving gloves, just staring at me. People told me he had been there looking at me for a long time before I noticed him. I told him I had to go to a team meeting and that was the last I ever saw of him.

I was older, but not much wiser, when I was coming back from a rally in Switzerland and the airport was closed because of heavy fog. The only way to get back to London was to take the train and boat. I got on the very crowded train in Geneva and walked up and down the corridor, looking for a seat. I saw a carriage with all the blinds down, peeped in and saw there were two young men inside. I opened the door and asked if I could come in. They looked me up and down and said certainly, and in I went. The train took forever, so at the end of the journey I had become very good friends with one of them. His name was Peter and he was in the British Army. When we arrived in London there was what they used to call a 'pea souper', a fog so dense you couldn't see a hand in front of your face. Of course there were no taxis running and my companion walked with me to a little hotel in Piccadilly, where Rootes always put me up when I was in London.

I saw quite a lot of Peter over the next few months and he even brought me home to meet his parents. Every time I was in England we would meet up, and he said it would be a good idea to get married. It was a whirlwind romance that ended as quickly as it began: he thought he was in love and I was sure I wasn't. He gave me a ring that had belonged to his grandmother to seal the deal. It was a scrawny little thing and not at all attractive. When I got back to Dublin I decided that I didn't want to be a British officer's wife and sent the ring back in the post.

I went out for a while with a journalist who wrote the William Hickey gossip column in the *Daily Express*. We were engaged and spent a lot of time in Ronnie Scott's Jazz Club as he watched the comings and goings of the current celebrities. That was great fun and I enjoyed the society life until the evening of a cocktail party in the Connaught Hotel in Mayfair. The party was rapidly running out of alcohol and so my fiancé said that, as he knew some Russians were having a party in the suite below and they would have plenty of vodka, he would ask them. He decided the quickest way to get to the floor below was to swing his legs over the balcony and clamber down. I saw him for the complete idiot he was and promptly terminated the relationship. There were others after him, but the romances never lasted long and I always made a point of returning the rings – that's only fair.

When I was in Ireland I loved taking part in the auto-crosses, a race where the circuit is laid out and cars compete against each other on grass, sometimes very wet grass. Slipping and sliding in a wet field and racing on grass is great fun. I was good at it, having had plenty of practice with my dad in our field as a child. It was at one of these events that I met my husband-to-be. It definitely wasn't 'love at first sight', but I was attracted to him. He was tall and dark-haired and seemed to be confident in himself.

Our first date, in the Horseshoe Bar of The Shelbourne Hotel in Dublin, didn't go well because he had just broken up with his fiancée and told me how badly it had affected him. I didn't want to be a shoulder to cry on, but I felt sorry for him and just listened – with hindsight I don't think he ever really got over her. We started going out together, as much as my rallying and racing commitments allowed; I always seemed to be off somewhere, and he had a business to run. Eventually, we became engaged in 1969. By that time I had achieved success in America, Canada, the UK, France, all over the place, and over time I think he became jealous and resentful.

We had decided we wanted to buy a house together, and when we were out one evening with friends in a pub we were talking about it. One of the men was an auctioneer, and after a considerable number of drinks he told us of a farmhouse for sale. We decided to go and see it there and then, semi-drunk in the semi-dark. In the twilight the house looked wonderful, a big square house with outhouses all around, and we shook hands on it. We went back the next day and I was horrified at the state of the place but saw it as yet another challenge.

The house, Macetown, was on 40 acres of land and was going for a song. No wonder it was going so cheaply: it had no bathroom and no running water, just a well in the middle of the yard. The man who owned it had 13 children and I don't know how they managed. My future husband said that it was the thing to do to live in the country. Not that he had any experience of it – he was brought up in Ballsbridge, Dublin 4. That's how it happened, I suppose; we had bought a house together, and financially it wasn't feasible for me to go it alone. The only sensible thing was to marry the man, which was the done thing at the time.

I made three appointments at the church to be married and it was only on the third occasion that I went through with it. I had no formal wedding dress and didn't want one. On the day I was to be married, on 28 August 1970, I went into town that morning and bought a pale green dress and jacket in Switzers of Grafton Street – nothing fancy, which was unusual for me. At the Church of St Peter's and St Paul's in Dunboyne, Father Ripson, the parish priest, asked me was I sure I was doing the right thing because he knew that I had changed my mind twice before. I really didn't want to get married, but I went ahead anyway.

My father stood outside the church when I got married. My mother didn't come at all; she said he wasn't good enough for me. She didn't like him in the beginning and made no bones about it, so, like many a daughter before and since, the more she protested, the more I just wanted to assert my independence and have a life of my own. Many years later, my husband ended up being very good to my parents and gave them both jobs, which they loved.

Terry Balfe, a lovely man who worked for Irish Shell, brought us to the Glenview Hotel in the Glen of the Downs for our wedding reception, and we went off for a few days' honeymoon with some of his friends and a man from Northern Ireland. There was very little romance in our marriage, but it was convenient. I continued my career and in between rallying all over the world I threw myself into trying to make Macetown habitable.

The first thing that had to be done was to knock down most of the existing building. When the builder came out with a big ball on the end of a chain to start work, before he began he asked had we got permission to do this? Permission? I didn't know I needed permission. I drove to the planning office in Dame Street and rushed in to get someone, anyone, to give me the required authorisation. The girl at the desk said it would take at least three weeks to get an appointment with the appropriate person. Just then that 'appropriate person' came out of his office and recognised me; I suppose I was at the height of whatever notoriety I ever had then and he was delighted to have the opportunity to help me. No doubt the story was told at many a dinner party afterwards. I explained my predicament and told him that the man with the wrecking ball was there ready to go, costing £180 per day, and I needed his go-ahead. He checked to see if there was a preservation order on the property, and when he found there wasn't he said that he would have to see the house personally.

We got in my car and drove to Clonee. He took one look at the house, decided it wasn't habitable and told the wrecker to work away on the demolition. The first bang nearly brought the whole lot down, it was so rotten! An architect friend of mine drew up plans and the work proceeded. The house that eventually emerged was stunning, with wonderful views from every window.

With the house completed, we had a proper wedding reception with around 60 guests, including Charlie Haughey and his wife Maureen. Although I had sent the invitation, I didn't really expect them to come and I was flattered when they arrived. Charlie Haughey was a leading Fianna Fáil politician, who went on to become Taoiseach no less than three times, and Maureen was the eldest daughter of Seán Lemass, a well-respected politician in his day. Maureen was a lovely woman and I worked alongside her for various charity events over the years.

We employed caterers for the occasion and there were drinks galore. Everyone had a great time and it was the beginning of a long period of entertaining friends and relations. The party was a success and everything went very well until we went into the little room we had put aside for the wedding presents. That room had long, low windows out to the garden, and when we went to open our gifts they were all gone. I don't know what people must have thought because I couldn't write thank you letters for wedding presents I had never seen. One guest asked me later whether I liked the dinner service she had given me; she was quite put out because she had taken a lot of time selecting it. Apparently, it was beautiful.

We were robbed again in that house when the thieves came into the bedroom, on the ground floor, and took the curtains and matching bedspread, which I had made myself, along with whatever valuables they could lay their hands on, including many of my trophies.

I regretted marrying my husband almost from the beginning. I think he was jealous of my career and he could not hide it. He couldn't deal with my success and it didn't help that in company people would call him 'Mr Smith', which really annoyed him. I never said I would give up my career when we married, so I never understood what he expected of me. I thought that being a successful driver was part of my attraction for him, but I must have been very wrong. He never tried to adjust to my way of life and got very sulky when my motoring friends came to the house. We would all be talking rallying – what went on yesterday, what was going to happen next week – and he just didn't want to join in.

We had rows and the next morning he would apologise, tell me how much he loved me and expect things to carry on as normal. I should have left him the first time I realised what kind of man he was, but I didn't have the courage. It's difficult for others to understand if they have never been in a disastrous relationship such as mine. When I was leaving to go on a rally, instead of wishing me good luck, he would say, 'Off on another ego trip?' He constantly put me down and undermined my confidence with remarks which I found hurtful. It makes me want to cry now as I write this because there is no way I would allow any man to speak to me like that today. What a fool I was!

There are so many instances of his cruelty but I remember Grosvenor House as being one of the most unpleasant. I was invited to be the guest speaker at Grosvenor House in London for a celebratory dinner for the racing fraternity. Graham Hill was there, along with many other well-known racing drivers of the time. Rootes were delighted that I had been invited to the event and told me to buy myself a dress, money no object, which I did. I bought a beautiful lilac Grecian-style gown, which went over one shoulder, tight-fitting with a train, and shoes to match. Vidal Sassoon did my hair and I thought I looked really well.

We were staying at the Grosvenor and as I came out of the bathroom, ready to go downstairs to dinner, my husband looked me up and down and told me I looked dreadful and that he always hated that dress, even though he had never seen it before. Stunned and humiliated, I cried and the tears ran down my face, ruining my make-up. I tried to pull myself together but I must have looked dreadful when I went down to meet everyone. I was supposed to make a speech but I just couldn't do it. It was one of the worst nights of my life.

For my birthday one year my good friend Cecil Vard, who had helped me so much in my early career, gave me a beautiful basket of flowers. My mother and father were horrified when in a fit of temper my husband kicked the flowers into the garden. But he wasn't just jealous of other men, he was jealous of my success and the attention that brought me. I was asked by a newspaper to take part in a competition, 'Whose smile is it?', but he felt that would bring me even more publicity. We had a terrible row the evening before the event and as a result I had to pull out.

There are so many times when he made my life a misery. I'll never forget that holiday in Tenerife when he accused me of flirting with the band. The men on the stage were dressed in Tyrolean costumes and were so small they would hardly have come up to my waist! I could tell you a million stories, but the outcome would usually be the same. 'Oh darling, I love you so much,' he would say the next day, 'we will never fight again' – until the next time, he should have said. I always say to the young girls I'm teaching in my driving school in Goffs, if your boyfriend is jealous, get rid of him right now. If they tell their parents, they probably think. Who is this strange woman? She's supposed to be teaching them to drive, not advising them on their love lives, but having gone through it all I know that jealousy is the most awful, ruinous thing in a relationship. I often asked myself why he wanted to marry me in the first place. Maybe he thought that I was going to make loads of money and keep him in style. Why didn't I leave him? I don't know. Maybe I thought that I had made my bed so I had to lie on it. It was 1970s Ireland, remember: I had nowhere to go and no confidence in my ability to manage on my own.

I have been pregnant four times and miscarried each time. One of those miscarriages was an ectopic pregnancy, which can be fatal if not recognised in time. I was taken to Blanchardstown Hospital and I was so ill that before the operation I was given the Last Rites. This was the nearest to death I have ever been, despite all my racing and rallying over the years.

I never wanted to have a child but my husband insisted that he wanted children and so we went to the Catholic Protection and Rescue Society of Ireland in South Anne Street to register to adopt a child. We were sent to a place in Gormanstown, County Meath, and brought into a room where there were babies in cots. The nun told us the ages of each of the children. My maternal instincts were aroused when I saw one little girl with the most beautiful eyes – eyes are always important for me – and I thought she could be the one. My husband had different ideas. He had picked out a redheaded boy, who, when I looked at him, screamed his head off. We signed all the necessary papers and produced the required documents. After a few weeks had passed I rang the adoption agency and asked when we would hear something about coming to collect the child, only to be told that my husband had telephoned them to say that he had decided against proceeding with the adoption. He hadn't bothered to tell me.

After some years at Macetown, my husband decided that anybody who was anybody was living in Dublin and so we sold our lovely house in Clonee and bought a town house in Eglinton Road, Dublin 4. We got very little for the farm, which I had made into a beautiful home, and the 40 acres of arable land. Had we waited a few more years we would have made millions, but there you go, that's the story of my life.

I was so unhappy in the new house. I hated it – I had to go to the very top floor to get a glimpse of the mountains.

The last straw was when my cat Blackie went missing. I loved that cat and searched everywhere for her until one day I had a call from Hughie, the man who had bought our farm: a cat had arrived at the house and he thought she might be mine. She was more brown than black, he said, and very thin and scrawny. I knew directly I saw her that it was my Blackie but Hughie wanted to be sure and asked me if she had any particular habits. When I told him that she would scrape her claws at the hall door window to get in and when the ashes had cooled down in the dog grate in the lounge she would curl up in them, we both knew it was her. Cats are funny that way: they seem to love their territory more than their owners, and Blackie had found her way back home.

Hughie's daughter, Mary, who had meningitis, had become so fond of her by then that I said they could keep her. I reckoned that if she managed to get back there once, she would do it again. I love animals and have had cats and dogs all my life.

So there I was in Eglinton Road with no cat, no mountains, and I was miserable. I saw a lovely old farmhouse in Kilternan, a few miles outside Dublin, and while I was away on holiday in Marbella I asked my husband to go and look at it and put a deposit down if he agreed with me that it was an ideal place for us to live. He rang to say that he was coming out to join me in Marbella, that he had bought the house and that my mother agreed that it was lovely. By this time she had settled her differences with him and they got on very well. He arrived with the brochure of the house he had bought, but it wasn't the one in Kilternan that I had looked at. Instead, it was 'Four Winds', a house on the Blackglen Road, Sandyford – the wrong house, the house that was to cause me so much grief, where everything went so awry and where in the end I had to get a priest to perform an exorcism.

It was a large bungalow and one side of the house had been built into the side of the mountains. It was designed like the letter 'H', with a little pool at the back of the house. A few weeks after we moved in, I fell into a huge manhole at the side of the house because the cover was off for some reason. That house brought nothing but bad luck.

When I had my last miscarriage, I was admitted to Mount Carmel and stayed in hospital for a few days because I was so weak. My husband hadn't come in to see me and I knew something was wrong because he always liked to make a good impression in front of my mother. She said that he had telephoned to say that he had gone out with the lads on Friday night and was hungover.

Despite my mother's protests, I insisted on being brought home that day; my instinct told me something was wrong. On the hall table I found a return ticket to London and I knew for sure he had been seeing someone else. It transpired that his former girlfriend was in London and he had been over to see her – she was the woman he had been engaged to before he met me.

Despite all of this I tried my best but in the end my husband was the one who walked out. We went to a solicitor, a separation agreement was drawn up and we parted. I was left poorer financially, but at least I was rid of him. Three years after, he got a divorce in Haiti and I was informed by an official letter. I put my own affairs in order when the ban on divorce was lifted in Ireland in 1996.

During this unfortunate marriage I continued racing and rallying. I suppose you could say I was well-known, in a minor celebrity kind of way, which my husband resented. I was away a lot of the time and my motoring friends kept me going, especially Pauline Gullick. She was one of the best co-drivers I ever had and our times together on the East African Rally in 1974 were unforgettable and a distraction from the misery of my marriage.

CHAPTER 12

RAINY KENYA

I HAD ATTEMPTED the East African Safari Rally in 1973, but that year I didn't get very far. I had been teamed with a very unsuitable co-driver, a young American girl with high heels and tight jeans who had never been in a rally before in her life. We only got as far as Aruba.

In 1974 my co-driver was Pauline Gullick, an excellent navigator and someone I had driven with many times. She was thrilled to be going to Africa with me, and as usual I was up for everything and anything. When Pauline heard I was recounting this episode in my book, she very kindly sent me some observations to assist my notoriously faulty memory. In her notes she wrote: 'I was amazed at Rosemary's skills in driving the car … it was incredible,' and she concluded, 'Thank you, Rosemary, for keeping me safe.'

In 1974 the Rally ran from 11 to 15 April. It was the first year the rally was run entirely within Kenya, and also that year it was renamed the Safari Rally. It was a 6,000-kilometre, five-day ordeal. The journey began in

Nairobi, from where we headed west through the Serengeti to the Victoria Falls, then east via Malawi to the coast at Mombasa and north again to return to the starting point. Since 1974 the rally has stayed within the borders of Kenya due to political unrest in neighbouring countries. Nairobi is traditionally the start and finish point, as well as being the midpoint where the rally's big loop stages meet.

We travelled by Kenyan Airways to meet up with our team-manager, Sidia Desai, who was working on our Datsun 1600SSS in the back streets of Nairobi with the rest of the mechanics. Sidia's father owned the Datsun dealership and most of Nairobi, from what I could see. Final preparations were being made to the Datsun to cope with the extreme conditions that it would encounter on the rally. By the time they had finished with it, the car looked very different from the cars I was used to driving in Ireland.

The Safari Rally is regarded as the toughest rally in the world, even in reasonable weather, but what we encountered in 1974 was unprecedented. The Kenyans had never seen such a wet season, and it rained in the desert for the first time in five years. Since its inception in 1953 the Safari has remained a road event as it is impossible to close a bush track and keep it free from all moving things except rally cars. The road is open to animals of all kinds, broken-down trucks, wandering buses or whatever might be on its way to somewhere else. It is not just a competition between cars and their drivers but a struggle with Mother Nature and the elements, as we soon found out.

We had two days in hand to do a recce and drove some of the stages to check conditions so that Pauline could make notes in the road book. The weather had been unseasonal and there were floods forecast, which threatened to sweep cars off the roads. When we did the recce, the weather was good and we were optimistic. You can never rely on the road being exactly as it was when practised as there are so many unexpected things that can happen, particularly the weather conditions.

We spent our first night in the Samburu Game Lodge, which gave us the unforeseen opportunity to meet some of the wildlife of Kenya. In the restaurant, as we ate our supper, monkeys joined us to share our food, while in the bedroom the large beds were taking up the whole of the room with mosquito nets covering them. I walked into the bathroom to see a snake writhing in the shower. I ran screaming to reception and the manager came back with his gun, only to find that it was a centipede and not a snake, which was a bit embarrassing. He took it away and we got to bed, although I don't think either of us slept very well.

The following day we continued our recce, and returned to Nairobi to make the final preparations for the start of the rally. The first section of the five-day event used the road from Embu to Meru around the eastern foothills of Mount Kenya, where there were torrential downpours severely affecting road conditions and we were in the middle of it all. The unrelenting East African rain meant that many of the cars didn't even get to the control and the ones that did were severely delayed. This section, which we had anticipated would take 82 minutes, was covered in 13 hours, 23 minutes! The only consolation was that weather conditions affected us all. Most of the entries were 10 hours late, even the best of them, including Roger Clark. The floods threatened to sweep cars and their occupants off the road and the mud made the going dangerous, with extremely deep drops on either side of the track.

Everything was gravel, dirt and dust until it rained, when it was turned into thick red gumbo mud; if you stopped, you just couldn't get going again – you would be stuck in the mire indefinitely. Cars stopped on the track, unable to move, and if we wanted to pass them they had to be bumped out of the way. So that's exactly what I did: I bumped them. I had a marker pen and I put a swastika on the side of our car every time we knocked one off the track, just like bomber pilots did in the Second World War. I think we ended up with something like 11 down the side of the car. People don't understand: you go out to win and you have to do whatever is necessary. I have always been told that I take rally driving too seriously – I don't know any other way.

Sidia and the team knew we would be encountering sludge and mud along the way, and so to combat that they had inserted a plate between the bumper and boot for the co-driver to stand on to help get traction. When we encountered roads which were reduced to running mud, Pauline did her best to jump energetically up and down on the plate at the rear of the car, while at the same time trying desperately to stay on board. A frightening experience for her, no doubt, but I just kept going, shouting encouragement from the safety of the driving seat.

There were times when the mud was so thick, even Pauline's frantic jumping didn't work, and we would come to a complete halt, stuck firmly in the mud. That is when the local tribesmen appeared, blocking our path and demanding 'push money'. The Masai tribe were very tall and thin, with long earlobes adorned with earrings, and they could be intimidating. But I wasn't going to let them know how threatened we felt and decided to resort to magic to frighten them. I revved the engine until the radiator was boiling, and even though I was terrified I got out of the car in the midst of the crowd, opened the bonnet, took the cap off the radiator and the boiling water gushed up like a fountain, scalding anyone approaching the car. The men ran off, terrified, looking back in fear and trembling at my witchcraft!

We carried bags of Kenyan shillings and, when we needed to, we could pay the local men to get us going again. Some of them just took the money and ran away, without giving us the push we had paid for. This was so frustrating until I got the bright idea to draw an x on the men's hands and told them that, once we were on our way, only those with the cross on their hands would get paid.

At the end of the first leg we had lost a lot of time, and although we should have had a 12-hour rest halt in Nairobi we couldn't afford to do so. If we were to stay in the rally, we estimated that we could only stop for 40 minutes. Exhausted, we lay down under canvas on the steps outside the Nairobi City Hall and slept. When you lose sleep like that, the mind plays tricks on you, and that's what happened to us the next night. The rain had stopped and we were driving along in the pitch-dark in the middle of Africa. Pauline was very quiet; I thought she had dropped off to sleep until she suddenly said, 'I don't know where we are.' Pauline, the most efficient navigator I have ever driven with, didn't know where we were! For some reason I wasn't worried, but continued to drive for miles, turning as we got to forks in the road in whatever direction seemed right to me. I remember we passed a tree with a noose hanging from it, which encouraged me no end to go even faster! Pauline never said a word because, as far as she was concerned, we were completely lost. She couldn't believe it when we arrived at the control, and neither could the marshals because they asked me how I had got there. I said we had recced the section and knew exactly where we were going, but Pauline knew that wasn't true; we hadn't been within 100 miles of the area on our recce. It was extraordinary and I felt then, and still do today, that something or somebody was looking after us.

Conditions on the second leg improved slightly. There were no mudslides, but in the middle of the night we came across a flood or, as I thought, a river with no bridge. After looking at the water for some minutes, I decided that we

Pamela, Lucette (co-driver), me, my mum and dad at the reception before the London–Sydney Marathon Rally

At the start of the London–Sydney Marathon in the Lotus Cortina

Khyber Pass 1968

End of the Marathon, happy me!

London–Mexico World Cup Rally
sign at Big Ben

Pre-London–Mexico publicity shot

Lord Stokes, Alice Watson and I at the start of the London–Mexico Rally

London–Mexico
with Alice Watson,
the Red Arrows
Team and Austin
Maxis, 1970

Alice, Ginette and I at the finish
of the World Cup Rally in
Mexico

In our striped Maxi on our
way to Mexico

In the Andes

Lake Caragh
on the Circuit
of Ireland in a
Ford Cortina

Circuit of
Ireland 1968,
3rd overall in
the Hillman
Imp

Rallying with
R.E. Hamilton;
Lombard and
Ulster in a Ford
Escort

London to Sweden to Monte Carlo towing a caravan for Europe by Europa

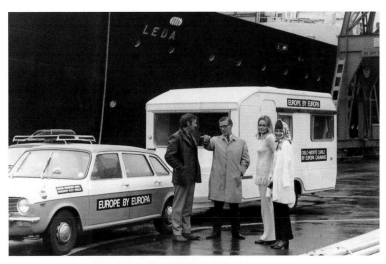

Some of my American racing rivals and I at Sebring, Florida

Pauline and I at the finish of the Safari Rally

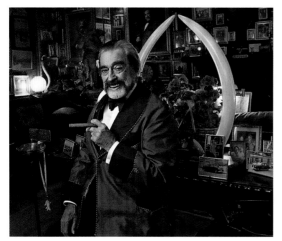

The flamboyant Peter Janson!

My very good friend Eileen Murphy and I at a charity ball

Mike Murphy presents a winner's garland after I beat him at a celebrity race in Mondello, 1967

Joann Bigger and I at Phoenix Park Motor Races

Mary Foley, now deceased, and I at a Ford launch

Pauline Gullick, Stirling Moss and I with our trophies at the finish of the Mitsubishi Marathon from London to Italy

Coupe des Dames winners, Historic Tulip Rally '92 – Pauline and I with our Sunbeam Tiger

With June Miller at the Renault F1 Drive at the Paul Ricard circuit, 2017

Having a drink with Pauline AFTER my Formula 1 drive

Being fitted into the Formula 1 car

With Alain Prost

Very glad it's all over!

could not attempt to go on until we knew exactly how deep it was. There was only one thing for it and I instructed Pauline to get out and take a stick and walk into the dark and murky waters that lay before us. For all I knew, there could have been crocodiles lurking in the black depths, but Pauline did as she was asked and walked through the water with a stick to check the depth. Between us, we decided we could make it through, although we took the precaution of having the windows tightly closed, just in case.

Due to all the delays we were running late in the rally, but all controls remained open for us as the bush telegraph had told the marshals that we were on our way. The tiredness was overwhelming as we went for days with very little sleep. It got so bad at one point that I started to see pink elephants walking across the track in front of us. I came to a grinding halt and Pauline asked why I had stopped. I said, 'Elephants,' and she assured me there were no elephants. This happened twice, and then on the third occasion I was not to be fooled again so I drove straight on, only to have Pauline yelling, 'Stop! Elephant!' I had been hallucinating before but this time the elephant was real and it was pink because it was covered in gumbo mud. That was a relief, but still my eyelids kept drooping as I fought to stay alert. I had lost one of my false eyelashes, which were my remedy for staying awake. Pauline had to rummage in the footwell of the car to find it.

On one section of the rally we had to drive through a valley, which was bordered by escarpments to the east and west. When Pauline directed me to drive up what looked like a very steep goat track, I argued with her and said that she must be wrong as there was no way the car could get up the steep incline. Some of our fellow competitors were attempting to get up. I took a chance and in the dark it was yet another challenge, which I am happy to say we successfully overcame. When we got to the summit we saw an arc of lights cascading down and discovered afterwards that it was a car falling backwards off the track.

Pauline and I were exhausted and very hot when in the middle of the desert the wheel got stuck in a very deep pothole. We knew we were the last car still running and this was probably going to mean that we were out of the rally, for which, for once, I said, thank heavens. Away in the distance I saw a man herding goats, and again my wonderful Pauline did as I asked and ran after him, shouting for help. The faster she ran, the faster the goatherd ran, and he just went further and further away. How long would it be before we were found and could get moving again? I looked up and saw a small plane overhead flying low and, miracle of miracles, it landed and two men got out and lifted us back on the road. Luck was on our side.

I will never forget those final miles driving to the finish in Nairobi. The route was lined with hundreds of people, stopping the car and cheering us on. The Kenyan women were giving us baskets of fruit; it was all very emotional and I certainly had a few tears when we reached the finish.

We were the last car home, and at the final control several of our fellow competitors were waiting to escort us into the finish at Nairobi Town Hall.

It is the custom for each winning crew to have their national anthem played as they go up to the podium. We went up to collect the Ladies' Prize to the tune of 'It's a Long Way to Tipperary'. The organisers obviously didn't know about the Irish national anthem and this was the best they could do. We didn't mind at all, we were just happy to be there. Out of 99 starters only 16 crews survived to finish. It was a great achievement and one of the most exciting events of my career.

That evening we telephoned our families to tell them that the rally was over and we were both safe and well. There was no telephone in our room at the hotel and we went down to reception to make the calls. When we returned to the room, all my jewellery and money had been stolen. This would have been a disaster but I had become very friendly with Sidia Desai and he came to my rescue. He insisted on getting a dress especially made for me to wear to the ball. The gown was incredible; it was a dark chocolate colour, silk, with embroidery and gold beading. We went shopping together and he wanted to buy me everything I admired. I was reluctant to take advantage of his generosity, even though I knew he was a very wealthy man. Sidia was charming and very persuasive. I admired a beautiful wooden carved chest, but I knew I couldn't bring that (or him!) home with me.

About six weeks after the Safari Rally I got a message from the North Wall docks in Dublin to say there was a delivery for me that I would have to collect. Intrigued, I drove to the docks and they very nearly didn't hand it over as I had no identification with me. One of the officials recognised me and said I could take it. The men put the huge package into the boot of my car. When I got home and unpacked it, you can imagine my delight when I saw the chest I had admired so much, brass fastenings and all.

The rallies all around the world were wonderful experiences and I loved every minute of them. As I said before, racing was where it was at if you wanted to prove yourself with the men. I always loved the thrill of racing and competed whenever I could.

CHAPTER 13

RACING AROUND

THE CRASH IN the Lotus Elan at Brands Hatch didn't put me off racing altogether, and when the Super Saloons was at its height in Britain I was there. Super Saloons racing, or 'Super Loons' as it was colloquially known, was an event where specially prepared saloon cars would compete. The prize money was good and the events were always well attended. My husband had sponsored Eddie Jordan in his rallying career and we were friends. Eddie started racing back in the 1970s at a professional level and went on to win the Formula Atlantic Championship. After retiring from racing, he founded his own team, Jordan Grand Prix, in 1991, where he gave many young drivers their first opportunity to compete, including Michael Schumacher.

Eddie was only at the start of his spectacular career when he helped me to get around to the various motor racing circuits in Britain. On one occasion we drove from Edinburgh to Liverpool, towing the Ford Escort, which was my 'super saloon'. We were both exhausted by the time we reached the outskirts of Liverpool and had no idea where we were going to sleep. I needed a good night's rest as I was racing the next day at the Aintree Motor Racing Circuit. We were short of money and barely had enough for petrol.

It was ten o'clock at night and Eddie pulled over beside a row of houses. He knocked on the door of one of them and asked for Mrs Grimshaw. When the lady told him there was no Mrs Grimshaw living there, he pointed at me sitting in the car and told her that I was racing tomorrow and we were sure Mrs Grimshaw was going to put us up. Eddie had such a way with him, he could charm the birds off the trees, and the woman looked at him and then at me and took us in. We slept well in separate rooms, and in the morning the lady of the house cooked us breakfast and refused to take any money, not that we had any. We gave her tickets for Aintree in return and went on our way. Eddie is a charming man who can talk his way out of every situation.

I have tried all sorts of ventures over the years, some more successful than others. When Bord Fáilte asked me to go to America in 1974 to promote Ireland as a tourist destination, I couldn't refuse. I was honoured, of course, but also a little reluctant. The only reason I agreed was because I thought my companions on that trip would do most of the talking. I was in illustrious company: David Cabot, environmentalist, ornithologist, broadcaster and writer; Jeremy Ulick Brown Altamont, the 11th Marquess of Sligo, who made his ancestral home, Westport House, into a viable tourist attraction; and Monica Sheridan, the TV chef and writer, much loved by Irish viewers.

We travelled first class with Aer Lingus to New York, a limousine was there to meet us and we went straight to the Waldorf Astoria, no less – such luxury! I knew all the best people stayed at the Waldorf, but nothing prepared me for the sight of the surrealist Salvador Dalí in a black mink cape, its red satin lining showing every time he swished it over his shoulder. He was talking to a crowd in the foyer of the hotel and there was a tall black girl to his left and a tall white girl to his right, and with his upside-down moustache twitching away I was mesmerised.

But we had work to do and I was disappointed when I found that David, Jeremy, Monica and I were each to go our separate ways. I had imagined that at least two of us would stay together the whole time. In the hotel, Joe Malone, Bord Fáilte's manager in North America, handed me my itinerary, wished me good luck and off I went to my first assignment in Boston. I thought we would have at least one night in the Waldorf and I might catch another glimpse of Dalí, but no such luck.

I discovered that persuading Americans to visit Ireland was not helped by the compulsory Shannon stopover. At that time every transatlantic flight had to touch down at Shannon Airport, and most visitors wanted to fly straight in to Dublin, the capital city. They didn't like the idea of wasting time on a stopover, they wanted to get the most out of their holidays. I had 14 cities to visit over the seven days of that St Patrick's week. Television in the US went on for 24 hours and my job was to go to the TV studios, do the interview to sell Ireland, and move on to the next place. What with the jet lag and the constant travel, I was hardly able to stay awake, never mind tell the Americans how wonderful dear old Ireland is. Driving and racing cars was easy work compared to this!

I did my best, but after three days of talking about Ireland I was feeling low and homesick. I was ready to take the next flight home and the only thing that stopped me was meeting Deirdre O'Callaghan in a country club on St Patrick's Day, where she was singing and playing the harp, as only she could. Deirdre was a big Irish and international star and the Americans loved her singing wistful Irish songs, especially 'When Irish Eyes are Smiling', and even though their ancestors had left Ireland a hundred years ago there were tears in their eyes. Her rendition of 'Raglan Road' was so moving that it nearly sent me running back to Dublin.

I was obliged to finish what I had started and I completed the job of promoting Ireland, but I was so happy when the time came to leave America. It had been a great experience being in the TV studios and I met some interesting people, but it would have been so much better if I hadn't had to do it alone.

At home in Ireland, I competed at Mondello, Phoenix Park, Dunboyne, anywhere there was a chance to race. In

1978, when the Irish Land Speed Record was up for grabs, Danny Keany and I had dinner together in the Milltown Golf Club and over a few glasses of wine we talked about setting a new land speed record, with me in a car and Danny on his motorcycle. At that time Danny was the sole importer for Yamaha in Ireland and a very successful motorbike racer.

Mick Hill, a racing driver from England, who was famous in the Super Saloon racing scene, lent me his Jaguar, which had a Formula 1 engine bolted in. He raced it all over the English circuits, which are mostly right-hand, so Mick had the car set up to go slightly to one side. The wheels had racing tyres fitted, which were smooth and perhaps not the best to deal with the ridged concrete of the Carrigrohane Straight in Cork. Someone said that if the drive shaft snaps, you'll be dead. I realised what they meant: the drive shaft was right beside me in the cockpit, and if it snapped it would fly up into my face and shoot me like a bullet from a pistol.

I nearly died before I even got there at all. The day before, I was on the Donegal Rally and my good friend Henry Martini offered to give me a lift in his two-seater plane from Letterkenny to Cork, where the event was to take place. He had flown up from Dublin to Donegal after the rally and landed his plane in a field. The rally had been delayed and it was getting dark as we took off. We were flying very low and it looked to me as if we wouldn't make it over the gate that was immediately in front of us. A farmer standing nearby must have had the same idea, because he got to the gate just in time and quickly swung it open; we managed to get through and up we went. If he hadn't done that, the wheels would have hit the gate and we would have crashed. The rest of the journey didn't go much better and my heart was in my mouth by the time we got to Cork.

The only acceptable place for the Royal Irish Automobile Club (RIAC) timekeepers to stage the event was the one-kilometre, perfectly flat stretch of road from Cork County Hall to Ballincollig, known as the Carrigrohane Straight. The Straight ran parallel to the River Lee on the right, and a public dump on the other side. Because we were so near the dump, seagulls were a problem and marshals on motorbikes drove up and down the road, shooting air pistols, to scare them away. It was a main road so it was closed off from 5.30 to 7 a.m. on the morning of 21 June 1978.

Danny and I drove up and back, and an aggregate was made of our speed. I went from 0 to 60 in a flash, and as I was driving over that ridged concrete road my helmet kept falling down over my eyes, so I had one hand keeping that up and the other on the wheel. I did well and for a few minutes I broke the land speed record, clocking 178 mph until Danny aggregated 185 mph on his 750cc souped-up Yamaha motorcycle and beat me. I hadn't really thought about wind resistance, and with the width of his motorbike against the width of the Jaguar, of course he was going to be faster. After two runs, one of the onlookers noticed my front left-hand tyre had an enormous bulge on it and if I had tried another run it would have burst. Someone up there was looking after me.

There were crowds there, even though it was so early in the morning, and as I stepped out of that Jag, took off my helmet, flicked out my long blonde hair and fluttered my false eyelashes, I felt like that one from Charlie's Angels! It was a great day for Danny Keany and an exciting one for me.

That same year I was asked to co-present a motoring magazine programme, *Motorways*, for RTÉ TV with Paddy McClintock. The producer was Peter Kenneally and the content of the programme was good, and I was fine when I didn't have a script. My problem was that I found it difficult to learn my lines. At the end of one session I was told to close the show with the words, 'The most important thing is to concentrate.' I kept getting it wrong, and in the end Niall Andrews, the director, got an idiot board so that I could read from it. Talking off the cuff is no problem, but don't give me a script or ask me to remember lines!

I was thrilled to be invited to host a TV talk show on RTE 1 in the 1980s. I was allowed to choose my own guests, which I did with care as I had never done anything like this before. It was a live show on Saturday night and I needed guests who could talk. My first guest was a then well-known young male fashion designer who was due to talk about the famous women he had dressed. He had also agreed to talk about his childhood and the abuse he had suffered. He wanted to let it be known that the abused should not feel shame for what had happened to them. However, when it came to the point when he was to talk about this he clammed up and would not speak. I remember the floor manager nearly had a heart attack. With 12 minutes left to fill on live TV I had to revert to talking again about designs and fabrics. Luckily, he had brought a number of large photographs of his designs worn by celebrities and we used up the time talking about those. Very sadly, years later I learned that he had committed suicide.

One of the guests I hoped to have on was Bill Cullen, who was just making a name for himself and had recently bought the Renault franchise in Ireland for £1. Bill had agreed to come on and had spoken to the producer Paul Cusack. But a few days before the show he pulled out because he thought that appearing on my show might jeopardise his chances of getting on *The Late Late Show*.

My other guests included Tony Kenny the singer, Bill Whelan of *Riverdance* fame and Marguerite McCurtain, who had hiked the Inca trail. My final guest was the legendary Paddy Hopkirk, who had invented a petrol can that would not burn or blow up if the car caught fire. Of course, a practical demonstration in the studios proved impossible. The rest of the show passed off in a daze and I was very glad when it was all over.

CHAPTER 14

FROM BAD TO WORSE

UNTIL THE EARLY 1980s I continued to drive in rallies as much as possible despite my husband referring to my endeavours as 'ego trips'. It was inevitable that his jealousy of me and my career would lead to the relationship ending. Despite all I had been through, I am sorry to say that my need to have a man in my life led me to yet another catastrophic relationship.

I wasn't exactly surprised when I got the letter from Haiti in 1988, telling me that I was divorced from my husband. It was a relief that I was free of him, although Irish law didn't recognise that until much later. He was free to marry again if he wanted, but not in Ireland. I was alone when that letter arrived, living in 'Four Winds', with my self-esteem at an all-time low. I had spent 20 years in a dysfunctional relationship and had little confidence in my ability to make a go of it with any man. My ex-husband had worn me down – some people learn from experience, but I wasn't one of them. Not then, anyway; it took me a few more years of living to get it right.

The evening I met my second partner, I had just come from the Mondello Park racing circuit and was sitting in the Manor Inn in Naas, having a drink and feeling sorry for myself. A man came over to my table and asked if he could buy me a drink. He knew who I was, but I had never met him before. He was a stereotypically tall, dark, handsome man and I suppose I was flattered. As I sat, sipping my vodka and tonic, while he told me how he had followed my career and how much he admired me, I thought of my ex-husband with his new woman and decided that a man in my life would be no harm. Little did I know …

He told me about his wife and their marriage break-up and my heart went out to him. Although he came from a wealthy background, he was not financially stable himself. The job he had as a salesman in a double-glazing company didn't pay well and he had to give part of his salary to his family. He was lonely, living in a small flat, and in my insecure state of mind I fell for it – and him.

It wasn't long before he had moved into my house and our life together began. I loved having a man around, and at first I was happy with my new relationship. After we had been together for a few months, he came to me with a proposition: he wanted to start his own company, making conservatories. Being a salesman in the double-glazing business wasn't for him, he wanted to be his own boss and make a good living for the two of us. The capital he needed for this venture was considerable and he suggested that I remortgage the house. Like a fool, I agreed.

All his grand plans didn't work out as anticipated. At enormous expense, he displayed his conservatories at the Ideal Home Exhibition in the Royal Dublin Society (RDS) in Ballsbridge. That didn't have the anticipated result and things went from bad to worse. As the business failed, his behaviour became more erratic.

It's no wonder the business didn't work out because when bills came in he put them straight in the bin without even opening them. You could always tell they were bills in those days because they came in cheap, brown window envelopes. People rang up complaining to me about half-finished or leaking conservatories. It came to a head early one morning, when the Gardaí arrived at the door and took him away. I didn't know exactly which particular bill had been ignored, or why the arrest was made, but I managed to get the £300 together to get him released.

Shortly after that, I suffered the humiliation of my name appearing in *Stubbs Gazette*, the publication that provides details of insolvencies and court actions taken against businesses in Ireland. An article appeared about the two of us in the *Phoenix* magazine, whose mission it is to 'inform, satirise, expose and entertain'. It is Ireland's answer to *Private Eye*, the British satirical periodical. I am happy to say that the *Phoenix* blamed him for the financial shambles we found ourselves in, but I was the one left with the debt. Some people took great delight in reading about my predicament – how the mighty fall and all that. Not that I can remember feeling mighty, not in those days anyway.

The premises he had in Ballymount were up for sale but nobody wanted them. Meanwhile, letters and bills continued to tumble through the letter box and there were constant angry phone calls, some of them in the middle of the night. When the conservatories developed cracks or roofs collapsed, his customers wanted their money back, and who could blame them? I was paying 28 per cent interest to the building society on the loan and there was no money coming into the house; I was desperate. One day he simply said that he couldn't take the strain any longer and walked out. He couldn't take the strain! What about me? I was the one left alone, up to my eyes in debt.

The only way out was to sell my home and pay off the creditors. It was a really beautiful house on two acres and well maintained. I was sure I would get a good price but I had left it too late because there were now plans to run a road through my property and selling would become impossible.

CHAPTER 15

ROCK BOTTOM

THE DÚN LAOGHAIRE-RATHDOWN County Council decided my property would be included on one of three proposed routes for the Southern Cross link of the M50. They hadn't made a definite decision at that stage, but told me that if they decided on the area in which 'Four Winds' was situated, then the road would be running straight through my bedroom. Obviously, potential buyers would be put off, but nevertheless I put the house up for sale and opened it for viewing. One prospective buyer offered me €2.3 million, but when they did their research and found that the Council had plans to run a road through the area they backed off, and who could blame them?

I looked for a Compulsory Purchase Order from the Council but they wouldn't grant one as they had not made a final decision. I kept telephoning over and over to see if they had made up their minds about where the road was going but it was no use, they were really unhelpful. There were days when it all got too much for me but I never let the house and garden go untended. I planted flowers in the garden and mowed the lawns myself.

The Dún Laoghaire-Rathdown County Council didn't run the M50 through 'Four Winds' in the end, but it took them 12 years to come to that decision.

In late 1996, soon after the Council had made their decision not to go ahead with their road plans, they announced their intention to put 20 families in 24 caravans on a site for the travelling community in Blackglen Road beside my house. It just didn't make any sense because the Council had repeatedly refused permission to have the entrances to the private houses opening on to the road on the grounds that the road was too narrow. I, along with the other residents, objected because the road was only 16 feet wide, without a footpath, and had the same usage as the Tallaght Bypass! I was concerned also because we were surrounded by gorse and fires occurred every summer.

The matter went to the High Court and the objections of the local residents were overruled. Letters appeared in *The Irish Times*, pointing out that it was proposed to spend €1 million on a halting site (a caravan site for travellers) that the travelling community themselves had described as a ghetto. An election was imminent and we lobbied our representatives. My neighbours and I decided to make a protest and sat on the road to prove it was not a suitable place for cars and caravans. The Gardaí were called to remove us, the newspapermen arrived and it was all great publicity for our cause. In February 1997 the matter came before the Supreme Court, when the previous judgment was overruled and a recommendation made that the proposed halting site should be located elsewhere. At least that catastrophe was averted and had provided a temporary diversion from my troubles.

My situation remained the same, and if I could have afforded bottles of wine I might have knocked myself out. I was penniless and all alone and I knew I had to do something to survive. I went to a small office in Cabinteely at the back of the church to a branch of the Citizens Advice Bureau. The woman I met there was Anna Kenny, a wonderful lady and to this day a great friend. She knew who I was, recognised me straight away, but she never let on. Anna just listened to me as I told her my position, with tears rolling down my face. After hearing my story, she tried to explain to me that there was no disgrace in receiving social welfare. I had always worked hard all my life and the idea of walking into a dole office was difficult for me, especially because I had been in the public eye for so long and would, no doubt, be recognised. The whole thing was embarrassing, but beggars without any food in the house can't be choosers.

Anna filled in all the forms and rang someone in the Dún Laoghaire social welfare office and let them know I would be coming. The official there came out of his office soon after I arrived and so I didn't have to stand in the queue for too long. Nevertheless, it was humiliating. I had been called upon to receive so many awards, cups and accolades over the years and now I was reduced to this. It was hard to take and I know I'm not alone; lots of people have to go through these indignities.

Receiving the social welfare was a lifesaver and at least I had enough to keep me going, but still, the future was bleak: I was alone, I rarely went out and many of my so-called friends had disappeared. I can identify with people I read about in the newspapers today, who are homeless or in debt through no fault of their own, because it is a terrible situation to be in. I don't believe I was suffering from depression – that's a clinical illness that can be helped with medication and therapy – I just felt hopeless and hated myself for it. It felt as if I couldn't do anything right. I suppose it's the same phenomenon that makes me remember the rallies that I didn't finish more than the ones that I did – I don't blame others, I blame myself.

One small lamplight was shining as I sat in the little conservatory one evening with my dogs beside me: Blackie on one side and Zac, my big Alsatian, on the other. All I had was a box of Maltesers and I was feeding them to the dogs, one for Blackie, one for Zac and one for myself. I looked at the fishpond outside and I thought if I went face down in that now, it would all be over in a few minutes – it would have been so easy. I had nothing to live for. People would say she was always a bit odd, we knew she would do something like that, and that would be the end of it. They wouldn't know what had happened in my life – as far as the general public was concerned, I was a success. Some of my closest 'friends' were no longer around; when all the parties stopped and the drink didn't flow, they just didn't want to know any more. I was thousands of pounds in debt with no hope of getting money from anybody and very soon the house was going to be repossessed. The only asset I had was my little car.

Those two dogs sitting at my feet must have known instinctively what was on my mind. Blackie put her paw on my knee and looked at me with her great big black eyes, while Zac nuzzled me. In that instant, I looked down at them and thought, the bastards are not going to get the better of me.

CHAPTER 16

LET'S FACE IT

ALL THE THINGS that had gone wrong in my life seemed to be reflected in my face: the failed marriage, the miscarriages, the debts, my mother and father gone, my brother Roger and sister Pamela dead prematurely, and now the trouble over my failed relationship and 'Four Winds'. My rallying career was over and I didn't regret one minute of it, but it had taken its toll. I had always been in the public eye for one reason or another, and now when I saw myself on television or in press photographs I cringed. I took to wearing high-necked tops to hide my neck and those jowls that I had inherited from my mother. I kept trying to think of ways to somehow reinvent myself, make some money and pay back the loans, but as I looked in the mirror at my wrinkles, I was in despair.

My low self-esteem was affecting every aspect of my life when my good friend, Eileen Murphy, told me that Highgate Private Hospital in London and the *Irish Independent* newspaper were offering me the opportunity to have cosmetic surgery. I don't know why they chose me. Maybe it was because at that time I was an ageing minor celebrity in Ireland and they thought it might be good publicity. In any case, I didn't question their choice and jumped at the chance, without knowing what exactly I was letting myself in for. This was a gift from heaven: cosmetic surgery, all flights to London paid, how could I refuse? If I had to pay for it myself, the cost would have been over £5,000, which I certainly didn't have. I had been unhappy with my looks for years and now here was a chance to rejuvenate myself. At 59 years of age I needed something to make me feel good when I looked in the mirror. Could this be it?

In November 1996 I went to London and presented myself for assessment by the surgeons. Cosmetic surgery was not widely available in Ireland and I knew very little about the procedure or the likely results. I asked some questions and learnt that plastic surgery had first been used in 1915 on soldiers who were disfigured in the First World War. The surgeons assured me that in the United States and the UK it was commonplace and I had nothing to worry about.

One of the surgeons was British and the other Indian, and between them they decided what procedures would be appropriate. The first man said he was going to cut around my ear, pull up the skin and remove the excess, giving me a smoother, leaner look; the other would perform surgery on my inner and upper lids, laser off the top layer of skin and remove three little moles from my cheek. The surgeons warned that I would experience swelling and that I would never be able to sunbathe again without a very high factor suncream. I asked when I could expect to see the results and I was told that it would take three months to heal altogether but that I could expect to see the difference in about six weeks. I felt I could trust them and agreed to go ahead without looking for advice elsewhere. In any case, I didn't know anyone who had undergone such a procedure. It's not exactly the kind of thing you tell your friends; people tend to keep it a secret.

My stay in hospital was scheduled to take three days. In early December I packed a few things and set off for what I hoped would be the start of a new life and a new face. For the first part of the procedure I was sedated, and I seem to remember that Beethoven was playing in the background, until suddenly my eyes opened wide. I had become fully conscious and I could feel the cutting of the skin around my ear. I was terrified and as I saw the look of horror on the surgeon's face he promptly put me under again. The second part of the treatment, my skin and eye surgery, was performed under general anaesthetic, so I didn't see or feel a thing.

In bed that night, I had to sleep sitting upright, with two pillows positioned under my head to help reduce the swelling. On the first day after the surgery I slept most of the time as the nurses smeared what felt like Vaseline on my face. Next day I was encouraged to walk up and down the corridor as a precaution against blood clots. I was miserable and even when Eileen telephoned I couldn't speak as my jaw was wrapped in bandages and I could hardly move it. For that reason, too, I couldn't eat but just sipped the nourishment they were providing through a straw. I kept asking myself, why had I done this and was I ever going to look and feel any way normal again?

Three days after the surgery the bandages were removed, and I could barely see. I was convinced that it had all gone terribly wrong. There was a stinging sensation all over my face and the stitches around my eyes were unbearably painful and itchy. When I looked in the mirror and managed to squint at my reflection, I was so shocked by what confronted me that I nearly fainted. The nurses were supportive and reassuring and said that this was to be expected. They reassured me that they were the normal side effects of the procedure and that I'd be right as rain after a few weeks. I wasn't convinced as all I could see were the swelling and blotches so I decided to stay at the hospital for a further two days – I just couldn't face the world outside that hospital looking like that. Of course, I had to leave eventually so I pulled myself together for my flight back to Dublin. Although I had a scarf around my face, dark glasses and a big coat with the collar turned up, the air hostess asked me if I had been in an accident. Accident! It was no accident, I had done this to myself deliberately, and I felt so embarrassed.

In hindsight, I should have stayed at the hospital longer. Back home in Dublin, the house was cold, I was all alone and missed the dogs, who were being cared for by my neighbour. I sat in the house feeling exhausted and very sorry for myself. It wasn't just the physical pain; I was in emotional distress and ready to cry at any moment. Worst of all, I knew that whatever I was feeling, it was my own fault: I had accepted the invitation to get cosmetic surgery and now I had to live with the consequences.

When I was in the hospital I had people around me, but now at home all alone I was miserable. I couldn't bear to look at myself and wanted no one to come near me. When I did force myself to look in the mirror, I was horrified by what I saw: my face was bright red and my eyes were emitting a horrible discharge. I telephoned the hospital for some comfort and they told me it was to be expected, but I wasn't convinced. The eyes became worse and I was frightened that I would lose my sight.

Half-blind and still wearing my big dark glasses, I returned to the hospital on 22 December to get the stitches removed. My eyes were puffed up and partially closed and they discovered that the cream I had been told to use on my face had got into my eyes and infected them; an antihistamine prescription helped to sort that out. Still, I looked a sight and would really have preferred just to go home in my wretchedness but I had been invited to spend Christmas Day with my good friend Pauline Gullick in Bristol.

Pauline met me at the station, and although she tried to hide her shock when she saw me it was written all over her face. She and her husband were so kind to me and looked after me with love and affection, which I sorely needed. Having lost my close family, good friends like Pauline are so important to me. She tended to the wounds on the back of my neck and helped me to see light at the end of the tunnel.

I went back to the hospital in February 1997 for the last time and by that stage was beginning to see the benefits of the surgery. A few weeks later I went to a dinner dance wearing a long, low-cut dress that I hadn't been able to wear for years because of my crinkly old neck. I was confident and felt attractive again. I enjoyed the admiring glances, which I hadn't had in a long time, and all the invitations to dance were gratefully received. That dance was the defining moment when I knew without doubt that having cosmetic surgery was the right decision. I wanted to look my best for as long as I could and I embraced the new, younger-looking me.

Does it sound shallow that I put so much emphasis on my appearance? I suppose it does, but I had always been known for my looks and that is a big part of who I am. I was convinced now I could do whatever was required of me to survive for the next chapter of my life.

CHAPTER 17

IN BUSINESS

WHEN I FIRST visited my sister Pamela after she moved to America, I was very impressed when I saw that her teenage children were being taught to drive at high school through a driver's education programme (Driver Ed). The grounds of the high schools in America are usually enormous and ideal for teaching driving skills, but unfortunately most schools in Ireland wouldn't have that facility. Although it took me a while to do anything about it, I became convinced that driving instruction for young people before they had their provisional driving licences would mean that there would be fewer accidents on the road. The earlier you get a young person behind the wheel, the easier it is for them to learn. I should know – didn't I do it myself with my dad in that field in Tallaght?

I approached several people in Dáil Éireann and met with little enthusiasm. I had a long discussion with Séamus Brennan, who had been Minister for Transport, and he listened patiently to my passionate plea for young people to be given this opportunity to learn the basics before they went on the roads of Ireland. 'It sounds like a great idea,' he said, 'but I'm afraid I can't help you.' I was very disappointed and was about to leave when he apologised again and asked me if I would be able to help him. Apparently Séamus couldn't drive and he wanted me to give him lessons so that he could pass his driving test. I did as he asked, but the irony of it seemed to escape him.

I decided that I would have to go it alone, so I did my research in the US and Europe, where it was normal practice, and set about developing what I called a Think Awareness Transition Year Driving Programme, suitable for young people in Ireland. Private instruction on private ground with qualified instructors meant that children could learn the basics of driving and road safety before venturing out on to the public roads. The three main things I required were the venue, backing from the motor trade and suitable instructors.

I went around to all my acquaintances in the motor trade in an attempt to get support and sponsorship but some of them turned me down flat and others couldn't get their heads around such a new concept. Eventually, I borrowed money from my friend Pat Doyle and started the Rosemary Smith School of Motoring in 1999. I approached Fairyhouse Racecourse because I knew they had extensive grounds, which they were not using all the time, and they were happy to accommodate me. Next, I sourced some reliable instructors, the most important requirement being that they could relate to teenagers. Keane Harley, a father himself, was an excellent classroom teacher, who understood how to explain the basics in a way that could be easily understood.

Together with some advisors, I devised a programme consisting of a one-day course for young people aged from 15 to 17, suitable for Transition Year students. In Ireland, Transition Year is a one-year programme taken after the Junior Certificate and before the two-year Leaving Certificate programme. The students do not need a driving licence as the lessons take place on private grounds away from traffic and the school provides comprehensive insurance. With help from Keane, a website was created: www.rosemarysmith.ie. (I am completely useless when it comes to computers despite the fact that I am constantly trying to get my head around them.) Before long, schools responded and the business took off. I worked so hard during the early years, travelling up and down the country to reach teenagers who couldn't get to Dublin for lessons.

For a few years everything went well until Fairyhouse had to rebuild the stands and needed the space. Luckily enough, I was able to move across the road to Tattersalls, who were happy to have us, until they too had plans for expansion and we were left with nowhere to go. I went to Naas, the Curragh and other racecourses to try and find somewhere suitable; eventually, someone suggested I try Goffs, and we have been there ever since. Goffs on the Naas Road in Kildare is Ireland's leading Bloodstock Sales Company with vast grounds and it suits perfectly.

I received support from Skoda and Ford for many years, but all good things have to end at some stage. Having driven Ford models for many years, I was sad when we parted company. I had met so many wonderful people during my time with them and the support they gave me was invaluable. But it was time to move on and some good journalist friends put me in touch with Renault, who asked me to become one of the Ambassadors for Renault Clio Ireland in 2016. They supplied me with a Renault Clio car to use in the school, and I am very grateful to them.

I love teaching the youngsters to drive and I feel that a lot of older people could do with some up-to-date tuition. Some of them don't know the new rules of the road, don't understand how roundabouts work and are confused by three-lane motorways. It worries me and I feel that everybody over a certain age should get tested. Young people are more inclined to listen; sometimes older people think they know it all. A very close friend of mine said to me one day that she knew she was probably the worst driver in the world but she had never had an accident. 'Yes,' I replied, 'but how many have you caused?' She wasn't just bad, she was dreadful, but refused to take up my offer of a lesson or two.

As I write, the school is still going strong and we have many students every year receiving their first experience of driving and road safety. I am very proud of that achievement and convinced that this early learning will make all those young people safer drivers in the long run.

CHAPTER 18

SEEKING SOLUTIONS

THE SCHOOL WAS going well and I had good friends around me at long last, but I still had the anxiety of living in a house that I was finding impossible to sell. I needed to sell to pay off the mortgage, and the constant worry of it all must have got to me. On Christmas Day in 2002 I was with my good friend Eileen Murphy and I felt exhausted. I thought maybe it was the fumes from the car I was driving affecting me, because it was my first diesel. But Eileen could see that it had to be more than that. She was working in the Blackrock Clinic at the time and told me to go for a check-up immediately.

At the clinic I met the cardiologist, Peter Crean, who is an absolute darling. 'How do you feel?' he asked me, and I replied, 'Tired, tired all the time.' 'Have you any pain?' he asked. 'No, but it feels like an elephant is sitting on my chest,' I told him. He put me on the treadmill but not for long, because he could see that I was becoming breathless very quickly. He said that I would have to have an angiogram straight away. The angiogram revealed that I had coronary artery disease, and two stents were inserted. I was discharged and told to take an aspirin daily and take things easy. Now, taking things easy isn't really me, and two days after leaving the hospital I was on a plane to attend a Historic Motorsports Show in Stoneleigh Park in England.

I enjoyed good health until three years later, when the same symptoms of tiredness returned, and I went to the clinic again. This time I was surely going to die, I thought. But no! The doctor inserted three more stents and I was alive and ready once again to try and sort out my ongoing financial problems.

Money was still tight; my mortgage still had to be paid, and with any start-up business there is little profit in the first few years. I couldn't understand it when one day I got a letter from the Department of Social Welfare to say that they had decided I was no longer eligible and payment ceased. I tried to plead my case to the department and my local TD (Member of the Irish Parliament), but was told I was not entitled to receive any kind of benefit. They even asked me if I had any offshore accounts. Offshore accounts? If I had them, that's exactly where I would have been, offshore!

As a last resort, I decided to ask Enda Kenny, who was the Taoiseach and leader of the Fine Gael Party in the Irish Parliament at the time, for his help. I had raced against Enda, along with Mike Murphy, a well-known Irish television personality, and Bishop Casey in a celebratory race in Mondello in the 1980s. I got on very well with him on that occasion, despite the fact that I won the race, so I decided to give it a go. I arranged to meet him in the Merrion Hotel in Dublin 2, which was just across the road from his office. I brought my bank statements and other relevant documents with me to substantiate my claim. Over a few drinks we had a great chat about old times, and I then proceeded to tell him all about my financial problems. He was most sympathetic and said he would see what he could do for me.

About three weeks later I got a letter in a white envelope with a gold harp on it from the Taoiseach's office. I was excited, until I opened it. That letter said that the Taoiseach has 'shown us your paperwork' and 'you are not entitled to anything', because they considered I had too much money. Well, they didn't say that exactly, but words to that effect. (I have friends who are married and very well off, who are getting pensions. I feel that it's totally unfair because I represented Ireland all over the world, but that doesn't count for anything.) All I wanted was to retain the social welfare money because, although I had started up the driving school, I still could not maintain my repayments of the mortgage without financial support. I had tried to explain that to Enda Kenny, but he and his department officials could not understand my predicament. I decided to take in a lodger, as my mother did long ago, and that eased the burden a little for the time being.

It was 2005 when Albert Gubay came into my life, or should I say I brought him into my life? I knew a bit about him – well, everyone did, he was famous. Gubay was a Welshman, an entrepreneur who made a huge fortune in supermarkets and real estate. He had made his name with Kwik Save Discount and went on to create supermarket businesses in New Zealand, Ireland and the US, and his current project was the Total Fitness chain of gyms. Gubay had bought the land behind my house and was going to build one of his gyms. I got in touch with him because I thought this might work in my favour: my house was so close to where the gym was to be, and maybe, just maybe, I could sell the property to him and this would be a way out of my debt to the building society. He agreed to meet me but specified it had to be at 8 a.m. the following morning as he was a very busy man. Eight o'clock in the morning is not the best time for me but you don't quibble over the time of a meeting with a billionaire. I got up early and had the coffee ready to go. That was my first mistake: he drank tea.

I explained my situation to him and said that it might be mutually beneficial if he bought my house as it was adjacent to the Total Fitness gym he intended to build. He drank his tea and seemed as if he was giving it some thought. I asked him how he had got involved with fitness, seeing as supermarkets were his thing, and he told me it was a bout of back trouble in the early 1990s that prompted him to venture into the leisure centre and fitness business.

The initial meeting went well but he didn't say yea or nay straight away. He invited me to dinner at Roly's Bistro in Ballsbridge a while later to discuss the sale of the house. Everyone knew him there and made a great fuss of him, and of course they knew me too, but the staff were very discreet. He was charming, when he wanted to be, and insisted that I ate broccoli because I had told him about the clogged arteries and the stents and he said it would be good for me. I got to know him quite well, and like many successful men he liked to talk about himself.

Gubay was very fond of his mother and I think it was because of her that he gave a fortune to the Catholic Church. He told me that when he was young and poor he made a pact with God and promised if he became a millionaire he would give half of his wealth to the Church.

Mr Gubay was a hard businessman, who didn't suffer fools gladly, and, as I came to find out, was ruthless in his dealings. He called to the house for tea many times after that and invited me over to his house in Wilmslow, near Manchester, a beautiful place beside a golf course. After some months of pussyfooting around, he offered to give me €250,000 for the house and a further €25,000 if I would petition the neighbours so that he could get the necessary planning permission to build the fitness centre and, most importantly, he offered me an apartment on the complex to live in for life.

I was desperate to get the house sold before the building society repossessed it, but in truth it wasn't the house he wanted but the two acres that surrounded it. So I trotted off each morning to talk to the neighbours and get their signatures on a petition saying that they had no objection to the Total Fitness Gym being built. I was pleased with myself as I managed to get the job done. I agreed to go along to the hearing with An Bord Pleanála, the national planning appeals board, and petition in hand to speak on behalf of the residents of the area. Gubay was there, of course, with his solicitors and colleagues, and I was surprised when, as I sat in the planning office, he didn't so much as look at me. When they broke for lunch, I got up to follow them out, but he ignored me and I realised my usefulness to him was over. When the hearing was completed and planning permission was granted, he walked out and I made my own way home.

I had agreed to sell the house to Gubay and in return, when I left Four Winds, he was to provide me with a rent-free studio apartment for life in the Total Fitness Leisure Centre. The mortgage was paid off, the building of the Leisure Centre was nearly finished, and he said I could stay in the house as a caretaker until building was completed. For some reason he changed his mind, and out of the blue he gave me three weeks to get out of my house after living there for 30 years. I protested and he extended that to three months to allow me time to sort out the house full of furniture and an accumulation of memorabilia, as well as finding accommodation, until I moved into the Leisure Centre.

I couldn't sell my furniture, although it was beautiful – the dining-room table was long, with 12 matching chairs; the sofas were huge and nowadays people in small houses don't need that kind of stuff. I telephoned the St Vincent de Paul Society because I thought they might be able to dispose of it and make some money for the charity. They came and took it away, but I was most upset when a few weeks later I got a bill for €300 for the removal of my furniture.

In 2007 I moved in with a friend until the apartment was ready. The apartment! I went to view the so-called apartment with my friend Pat Doyle. It was number 116, I'll never forget it. When we opened the door, we found it was just one room: 25 square metres, with not a cupboard in sight. It was positively claustrophobic. I couldn't possibly move into that for even one day, never mind the rest of my life. Mr Gubay had to be joking. But he wasn't! It transpired that the so-called apartment was part of a sports science complex, designed as a dormitory-type building where athletes could stay for short periods. It certainly wasn't suitable for a 70-year-old woman with a houseful of possessions.

I went to my solicitor and started proceedings against Gubay immediately. It turned out that government regulations required 'apartments' to be at least 45 square metres and also the planning permission did not allow for permanent residential use. He had planned for international athletes to stay there and train in the gym for short periods, which was perfectly legal, but permanent accommodation was out of the question. Gubay had pulled a fast one on the wrong woman! I began proceedings and took him to the High Court, where I was granted damages. What with paying solicitors, storing what was left of my furniture and finding somewhere to live, the next few months were difficult, but at least the liability of the mortgage and the arrears was off my back.

After some months I eventually rented a house in Sandyford. When I moved, I thought I would never settle into the small house with its tiny garden, but now I wouldn't leave it. I feel safe here and my neighbours are very good to me. I have a small circle of loyal and supportive friends and I am happy. Mind you, I often say it feels as if I lost 15 years of my life with all my troubles but that makes me only 65 now, so that's OK. I enjoy living alone and being able to do my own thing whenever I want. I have my work at the driving school and I am always being asked to go here and there to motoring and other social events. When I am at home, I have the radio and television and I adore the soaps and the Discovery Channel. I was never a great reader because I get so easily distracted. I would like to have a dog or a cat, but I am away too often and it wouldn't be fair. I once had a dog called Mossie, who would get into my suitcase and hide under the clothes whenever I was packing to go away.

I consider myself very fortunate. I am debt-free, not a rich woman, but a contented one. This thing of looking back and having regrets is not for me. You can look back on good things and be happy, but if they're bad things, what is the point? Albert Gubay once said to me, never have regrets, there is nothing you can do about the past. That was the only thing he was right about as far as I am concerned.

CHAPTER 19

RECOLLECTIONS AND REGRETS

I HAVE VERY few regrets, and those I have I try not to dwell on. When I reflect on the past, it's mostly the happy times I remember, and all sorts of weird and wonderful happenings and people come to mind.

Liquorice Allsorts and Winegums were my sweets of choice when I loaded the car before setting off on a rally, as well, of course, as the obligatory glucose tablets. On the marathon rallies I always had a bottle of water attached to the car, with a tube coming out of it so that I didn't have to take my hands off the wheel when I was thirsty. I wore a crash helmet on special stages but I had a selection of hats too because when I pulled off the helmet it would mess up my hair and that wouldn't do. I wore the customary, specially designed driving gloves, not only for increased grip, but also for protection against heat and flame. Nowadays I wear soft leather gloves when I am driving. No matter how long a rally was, or how exhausted I became, I always ensured that when I stepped out of the car at the finish I looked the best I possibly could – I was known for it.

It's funny the questions I get asked when I am going around the country, giving talks, and one of them, usually asked by the women, is how did I manage on the long-distance runs to go to the loo? I tell them, with the greatest of difficulty, but it is just a question of going where you can. You're not going to find a portaloo at the top of the Khyber Pass or high up in the Alps, so you have to make do. Of course, the difficulty is that a lot of the driving suits have zips from the neck down to hip level and you have to struggle to get out of them. When you are in a rush and out to win, you don't care if men in their rally cars pass and toot at you, so be it.

I was beating the men in the 1960s, when women were often considered arm candy in motorsports. But I wasn't stupid enough to think I got the drive on my ability alone: I was the blonde 'dolly bird' who grabbed headlines for the motor industry, and some men resented my success. My confidence was continually undermined. 'What are you doing here?' they would ask when I turned up for team meetings, and I had to stop myself from apologising for being there at all. It did get to me on occasion and there were times when I thought, maybe they're right, I shouldn't be driving with the big boys. But it wasn't easy. When I did well I would get remarks hurled at me, like, 'Did everyone else fall out?' and 'Aren't you lucky you won that rally? You must have the best car.' The truth was that I was rarely given the 'best car' because they were kept for the men. That changed somewhat when the competition managers realised that I was beating the men and winning rallies.

My driving days were not confined to racing and rallying. Crowds stood on the edge of the road in the middle of London when the British Minister for Transport waved me off with Alice Watson beside me in September 1970. I had only been married a few weeks, but this opportunity was too exciting to pass up. This is my usual reaction when invited to do something mad or unusual: I jump at it. I had been asked to tow a caravan from London to Sweden, following the Monte Carlo Rally route over the Alps, as a publicity stunt to promote sales. I had never towed a caravan before, or anything else for that matter, and on the day I had only one hour to practise. I was driving an Austin Maxi with 'Europe by Europa' emblazoned on the side of it as I towed the four-berth 16' Europa 390 caravan on the Oslo to Monte Carlo Rally route. The advertisements proclaimed: 'Buy a Europa caravan and win the Monte.'

We drove up Oxford Street, in rush-hour traffic, before hitting the M1 to Harwich, boarded the ferry to Oslo, and that was where the fun started. The PR manager and the managing director of the caravan company were in a car coming behind us in case of any emergency. Once we were in France, there was no snow as there would normally be on the Monte Carlo Rally, and the only problem was that a lot of people were on holiday and the roads were extremely busy. Trying to pull a caravan around all the twisty roads, with traffic holding us up or coming towards us, was tricky. We could hear the loud bangs, when the contents of the caravan fell around, as we negotiated the bends. I might have been going a little faster than the average driver with a caravan, but we just carried on and hoped for the best.

We slept in the caravan until we eventually arrived in the Metropole Hotel in Monte Carlo, where we were to stay overnight. As it happened, the two men who accompanied us were charming, so we decided to stay in Monte for a few more days; well, the weather was lovely too! The caravan was taken back on a trailer so we were free of it after that. The sun was shining and I knew back home in Ireland it was raining. We accepted the invitation to stay for a few days and we were glad we did. We sunbathed, drank the best of wine, enjoyed the food, the delightful company, and stayed in the best hotels.

When I was rallying, staying in nice hotels for any length of time just didn't happen; the accommodation was usually very basic, and that's why I jumped at the offer on the Tour de France Rally (nothing to do with the cycle race, of course). The Tour de France was a brilliant event that started in 1899, four years before that famous bicycle version, and, as its name implies, was a car rally run over French mountain climbs, where competitors raced at each of the major race circuits.

When we arrived at the circuits, enormous marquees – one for men and one for women – were erected. There was a very well-to-do French girl driving a Ferrari and when she saw me going into the marquee with the other women drivers she came over and, in very good English, asked if I would like to share her tent. I looked over at her 'tent', which was like no other I had ever seen; it was dark green with a golden metal trim around it. I had been told that she was a multi-millionaire and she certainly looked the part – beautiful and glamorous.

I took one look at the enormous marquee my colleagues were already entering, and another at her beautiful gazebo. Naturally, I followed the French girl. Inside, there was a separate bathroom with a shower and everything was so plush and luxurious, with beautiful red velvet covers on the beds and a chandelier. Having driven on the hot roads of France for a day and a night, this was heaven.

She told me I could shower first and I came out of that bathroom in my bra and pants, smelling wonderful and so happy with myself. She smiled as she came towards me, took me in her arms and started to kiss me. I wasn't expecting that and I screamed, pushed her away and rushed out of the tent just as I was, half-naked, grabbing my clothes on the way. As I burst out, there was a group of lads sitting there, laughing their heads off. 'We wondered how long it would take you to cop on,' one of them shouted after me. Apparently a male driver had tried it on with Mademoiselle and she had told him where to go. I heard she later married a gay man who owned a vineyard adjacent to her own.

Far from France, I had great fun working with the Lombard & Ulster Bank in Northern Ireland when they were sponsors and R. E. Hamilton supplied the Ford Escorts. The managers of Lombard were clever and knew that, to get publicity, presentation was key. They took us to the Jaeger shop in Belfast and bought outfits for the whole team, men and women, and we looked incredibly smart. I would love to be able to walk into Jaeger now and have anything I put my eye on paid for.

Pauline Gullick and I took part in many rallies for Lombard & Ulster in England and Scotland. The two-day event on the Isle of Mull, which is the fourth largest island in Scotland and renowned for its spectacular scenery, was particularly memorable. In 1968, while on a family holiday at Glengorm Castle near Tobermory, the late Brian Molyneux had the idea of holding a rally on the island. Brian was a Lancashireman and chairman of the Mullard Motor Cycle and Car Club in Blackburn and enlisted his fellow committee members to help in the endeavour. It took a while to persuade the islanders, but eventually the first Tour of Mull took place in October 1969.

The Tour of Mull Rally in 1972 was particularly memorable for two reasons. The first is that I was 4th overall and I believe this has not been achieved since by an all-female crew, and secondly, because of a man. I won't mention his name, but this gentleman had for some reason got 'a bit of a thing' for me. We stayed in the hotel on the jetty, and every time the ferry came from the mainland flowers would arrive – it was like a floating floral display! It was October and those flowers must have cost a small fortune. I gave them all to the hotel and the manager was delighted to be able to display them in every room. As for the admirer, well, it was a long time ago!

More recently, I was honoured to see myself on a post-age stamp. To mark the centenary of the Royal Irish Automobile Club in 2001, An Post, the Irish General Post Office, issued a set of four stamps depicting various aspects of Irish motorsport. The stamps showed Paddy Hopkirk in his winning red Mini Cooper on the Monte Carlo Rally in 1964; Damon Hill winning the 1998 Belgium Grand Prix; a 1929 Mercedes SSK in the Irish Grand Prix in Phoenix Park; and me in the Hillman Imp on the Tulip Rally in 1965. That was really great and I have the whole set of stamps framed and sitting in pride of place in my home.

I have met many famous people in my career. Clement Freud was someone who crossed my path in the 1970s. He asked to meet me on one of his visits to Ireland, when he was staying in the Gresham Hotel, one of the best hotels in Dublin at the time. Horse racing was a passion of his and he once lost 30 pounds in weight, so that he could become a jockey. That was a short-lived career and by the time I met him he was the portly gentleman, who achieved fame by cooking, talking and being in an advertisement for

I was honoured to see myself on a postage stamp

Chunky dog food with a bloodhound called Henry. They say that owners of dogs end up looking like their pets and he certainly did have the look of a hound.

He was with Hugh Hefner in the Gresham on the day I met him. Freud was involved in the London Playboy Club and had met Hugh in Chicago, when he was writing for *Woman* magazine and following the story of six British girls who had gone out there to be 'bunny girls'. I had nothing in common with either Hugh Hefner or Clement Freud, but Clement took a fancy to me and brought me on a number of lecture tours in England. I don't know if he liked me or if he thought that my lack of education might benefit from his superior intellect! I was glad I didn't get too involved, considering what was revealed about him after his death.

When I gave up rallying full-time, I was invited to become an honorary president of many motorsport clubs, at home and abroad. It was an honour to be asked to go to New Zealand, where the people are so friendly and the scenery is amazing. You could drive for miles and miles and see no one, just beautiful green fields, mountains, lakes and sheep. We were travelling one day on a classic rally and we stopped for tea. We were the only car for miles and suddenly a little Morris Minor went by, and the woman, who was putting the teapot down on the table, said, 'It's rush hour in Piopio.' There are only 400 people living in that town and I suppose two cars passing in an hour constituted heavy traffic!

I don't travel now as much as I used to and find myself fully occupied at home in Ireland. I have many acquaintances and a handful of very good friends, who I see all the time. They are of all ages and I find the age gap doesn't matter any more, thank goodness for that! The young people at the driving school call me Rosie and I think it's great – I grew up in a time when you couldn't speak like that to your elders.

Young people today are full of confidence, and in the 19 years I have been running the school I have seen that grow and develop. When I ask them what they want to be when they leave school, they are full of ambition, with dreams of becoming vets, doctors, pop stars, scientists and writers.

Most of them will go on to college and I envy them because I never had any formal education (my fault entirely). I know what's going on in the world because I keep myself well informed, but I also know that I have missed out. I have to admit that my lack of a proper education is a regret.

I have every admiration for young women today as they embrace the many opportunities open to them. Those opportunities were denied me when I was young, not that I ever let that stop me. I operated in a male-dominated industry and had to prove myself every step of the way. From 1933 in Ireland, there was a ban on women working once they were married, and this ruling was in place for 40 years. If you worked for the local authorities, health boards or civil service, your employment was automatically terminated once you married. Women were supposed to stay at home and look after their husbands and children. These days many men stay at home to be stay-at-home dads, while their wives or partners go out to work, and they are happy to do so. When I was young, there were very few women working in science or engineering, and that is changing now to some extent. In politics, women are beginning to take their rightful place too. We have had two women presidents here in Ireland: Mary Robinson and Mary McAleese, who were both very successful. Currently, there are women leaders of political parties worldwide: Chancellor Angela Merkel in Germany, Prime Minister Theresa May in the UK, Governor-General Dame Patsy Reddy in New Zealand, President Kersti Kaljulai in Estonia.

These women all hold positions that in the old days would have been occupied exclusively by men. The only area absolutely closed to women is full participation in the Catholic Church, but with its current attitude that's no loss!

Young women today can make up their minds what they want to be and follow their dreams. They shouldn't let anything or anybody stop them and if it doesn't work out then they can go on to something else. When a young person fails the driving test and they are upset, I always tell them not to be disheartened and not to say they have failed. They haven't failed, just not passed this time, and they have gained more experience for their next attempt.

I was helped and encouraged in my career by my father. He was a gentle man and all my memories of him are good ones. If not for my father's encouragement when times were hard, I might have given up. He was my champion and I wanted him to be proud of me. He had driven in the Phoenix Park races as a young man and the idea that his beloved 'Bub' (that's what he called me) had the opportunity to succeed in the sport was for him a dream come true.

My relationship with my mother was so different. Jane Kavanagh was a complicated woman, talented in so many ways, yet never content. She didn't hide the fact that my brother Roger was her favourite. Why wouldn't he be? He had such a lovely disposition. I am sure my mother loved me, but you would never know it from the way she sometimes behaved when we were together. No matter what I said or did, she would make something of it. Why do you wear your hair like that? That dress does nothing for you … On and on she went, with her negativity eating into me until I would walk away in despair. In company, she would answer questions addressed to me, as if I wasn't clever enough to answer for myself. If she was here today, I know she would be giving me instructions as to how to write this book! It must have been something about me that brought out the worst in my mother because I know my cousins thought she was wonderful and my father adored her. I got on splendidly with my dad and he and I could spend hours together with never a cross word; he was my rock and I worshipped him.

I have been thinking a lot about my mother and it occurs to me that her discontent might be due to her upbringing. My grandmother died at the age of 28, when my mother, her sister Lily and their three brothers were very young. My grandfather remarried very quickly and had four more children with his new wife. Although my mother and her siblings were not exactly neglected, they were put to one side. Their stepmother was more concerned with her own children than with them, and the nurturing my mother must have craved was missing. She worked in her father's company, but after marrying the only time she worked outside the home was when she and I ran the dressmaking business. Into her old age she would justify this by saying women didn't go back to work after marriage in her day, but I believe her affair with my father's friend had more to do with it.

Towards the end of my mother's life, when my sister was in America, my brother Roger, my father and her second husband were all dead, all she had left was me. She lived about two miles from my house, and every single day she telephoned to ask where I was going and what I was doing. When I brought her out to lunch with my man friend, she started a row over something and tried to get him on her side against me.

I never took her outbursts lying down, but tried to stand up to her, and it all came to a head one Sunday. We were out on a drive in Wicklow and she began her usual string of cutting insults and criticised my driving. I got angry with her and she accused me of having no sense of humour. I can hear her now, talking and wittering on until something came over me. I shouted at her to stop, but she just kept on and on, so I pulled over on to the side of the road at Rathdrum and I told her to get out of the car. She must have thought I was joking at first because she sat there for a moment until I screamed at her: 'Get out! I can't stand it any more and I might kill you if you don't go.' With that, she picked up her gloves and bag and calmly got out of the car.

I drove home at top speed, not pausing to think about what I had done to my mother. Once inside my front door it hit me, and I started to imagine all the terrible things that might happen to her. What was I thinking of? What had I done? I got in the car and drove back down to where I had left her, but she was nowhere to be seen. I drove backwards and forwards and I knew she couldn't have gone far.

There was a little café by the side of the road and I went inside to ask, had they seen an elderly woman with white curly hair? 'Yes, she was here and they all had tea together,' the woman told me. 'Who were they, do you know?' I asked. 'I don't know,' came the reply, 'but they seemed to know her and they said they were giving her a lift home.' I went home and didn't expect to hear from her again in a hurry, but next day she telephoned as if nothing had happened. It was all lovey-dovey: How are you darling? Will we go for lunch today? I would have preferred it if she had called me a thundering bitch for what I had done. My mother had minded me through my miscarriages and bad times, and we should have, could have, been the best of friends, but it wasn't to be.

My mother had a brain haemorrhage in 1986 and was admitted to St Vincent's Hospital, where the doctor told me bluntly that it would be better if she died as she would be a vegetable if she survived. I stayed by her bedside into the early hours, until the nurse said I should go home and get some sleep. Two hours later, the telephone rang and I was told she had died. I should never have left her to die alone; she would never have abandoned me, I know that, and I have regretted it ever since.

CHAPTER 20

DÉJÀ VU

I AM STILL being invited to drive in classic and historic rallies, and I rarely refuse. Why would I? The idea behind these rallies is to relive some of the great events of the 1960s and 1970s, celebrate the cars we drove over long distances with little support, and then there's the added bonus of meeting up with old friends. Because there is no pressure and plenty of help if things go wrong, reliving those rallies can be tremendous fun, most of the time.

Classic rallies are held all over the world. The Western Australia Classic Rally was established in 1992, and in 1994, when the first international entries were included in Perth, I was nominated to be the Driver of Honour. Perth is a beautiful city and I was delighted to be invited. I was told my navigator would meet me at the airport. I duly bought a bottle of Irish whiskey and a side of smoked salmon as a gift for the family. Unfortunately the lady of the house told me that they didn't drink or eat fish! That was a bad enough start, but when I saw the state of the

Hillman Imp I was supposed to be driving in a few days, I nearly turned tail and went home again.

My navigator was to have the car ready, and when I saw a wreck of a vehicle sitting up on blocks with a wheel missing and the other three not looking so good, I was shocked. 'Don't worry,' he assured me. 'I'll fix it in time.' I knew that was impossible but I said nothing and hoped for the best.

Our first engagement was a reception in Perth city. Once there, I confided in some of the officials that the car was missing a wheel and the engine obviously hadn't been turned over in ages. People were trying to help and some-one said they had spare parts but there were no tyres to be had.

I was naturally very upset because I had been brought all the way from Ireland to find myself with no car to drive. The young man in question was nice enough but he knew nothing about cars and he certainly wasn't a rallyist. The press reception the next day was held in the Mazda Brooking showroom and by this stage I was ready to abandon the drive altogether. All the press were there and when they asked me what car I would be driving I told them that I didn't know but it certainly would not be the Hillman Imp because it wasn't ready. The young man wasn't happy, but it was the truth and there was no getting around it. When the people who owned the showroom heard what was happening, they agreed that it was a ridiculous situation and insisted on giving me a brand new Mazda.

I arranged to meet my young navigator at the start of the rally, a few days later. We were meant to be starting number one car, but he arrived late and he had forgotten his shoes and I don't know what else. I was livid and didn't even want him with me, but it wasn't allowed to leave your co-driver behind. We eventually started off and I had to keep asking him which way next. This is not what you expect from a navigator: they are supposed to give you direction. I thought it strange that there were no checkpoints along the way to stamp our cards and discovered why when we reached the first time point. Although a number of cars had started in front of us, when we arrived nobody was there. The checkpoint hadn't even been set up because we had arrived an hour too early! Instead of following the prescribed route, he had just guided me by the quickest way on his map. I didn't know whether I wanted to murder him or burst into tears. An official came along and I explained that we hadn't gone to any of the checkpoints along the way. They overlooked it, because they could see that my navigator hadn't got a clue. I suggested we follow one of the other cars after that fiasco, but it wasn't a pleasant trip as he was sulking at this stage.

During the rally there were a number of special fun stages, and one of these was a two-mile circuit in a loop. We were the first to start, and my navigator, true to form, sent me in the wrong direction from the off. We should have taken the first left, but he told me to go right and when we got halfway up I saw that all the sign boards were pointing in the opposite direction. Suddenly, all the officials were waving us down. We were coming in the wrong direction and everything came to a grinding halt as I tried to extricate us. When we got back to the start, they wouldn't let us do it again and I really didn't blame them.

I am telling you all this to justify what I did in the end to my so-called navigator. A crowd of photographers were gathered, waiting to get the best shots as the cars arrived. At the end of another disastrous run I pulled the car up beside the photographers and told the young man to open his door. As he did so, I lifted my leg, kicked him in the beam end and booted him out of the car. He landed on his hands and knees in the gravel and all the cameras were snapping. I was so angry with him because we had this beautiful, powerful Mazda, which was so easy to drive, but he had ruined everything. Well, not quite everything, because we had a few driving tests with big open spaces and cones to be driven around, which was brilliant, great fun, and I did very well. I met him some years later and he was married with two children and he had by that time got the Imp in good order as he drove it from Perth to England.

One thing about my time in Perth I will never forget was the opportunity to meet some young people suffering from cancer, who were fundraising for a society called CanTeen. CanTeen is an organisation serving young people between the ages of 12 and 25 who are suffering with cancer. They were a wonderful group and I got very friendly with one young woman, who was mad about cars. We corresponded for a while until one day her letters stopped coming. I wish I knew what happened to her and can only hope she is well and free from that dreadful disease.

I drove a Sunbeam Tiger in the Mitsubishi Classic Marathon of June 1992, and it was a memorable event. Over six days the route went through Holland, Belgium and Austria and finished in Merano, in Italy. Stirling Moss was there that year, driving an Austin-Healey 3000, as well as Mike Cornwell and Anne Hall. The biggest challenge was the infamous Stelvio Pass, the last hill climb of the rally, which has 48 hairpin bends, and in some places the road is exceedingly narrow.

In a rally you can win or lose on a card stamp, and as we approached the control at the top I was so anxious to make sure we got our card stamped in time that I practically pushed Pauline Gullick, my long-suffering co-driver, out of the car. Although it was summertime, the snow was thick on the ground. There were two other girls driving an MGA and the competition between us was fierce. They were in the Royal Navy and I believe they had been living together for a long time. The rally was handicapped and as they had the smaller engine we had to catch them by 1 minute and 30 seconds on each stage. We beat them by 28 seconds overall, driving our Sunbeam Tiger. At the end of the climb, on the top of the mountain, we all got out of our cars and the nicer of the two came over to say well done. Across the snowy mountain top a spanner came flying towards us, thrown by the co-driver; I don't know if it was meant to hit her or me!

I did that Classic Rally again in 1993 and 1994, and when David Duncanson, a Scotsman with a lifelong passion for the Tiger, asked me to attend the Tigers United USA meeting in 1997, I jumped at it. I knew nothing about the Club, but was soon to find out.

The first Tigers United was held in 1974 in Grants Pass, Oregon. It was established by Bruce Fountain of STOA (Sunbeam Tiger Owners Association). It is quite extraordinary how enthusiastic Sunbeam owners are about their cars.

The Tigers United meeting in 1997 was an amazing experience and brought me to the attention of the Americans in a big way. Ian Hall, former assistant competitions manager for Rootes, and I were invited to attend as special guests. It was arranged by David Duncanson and Norman Miller, an American and author of *The Book of Norman*, considered by many to be the last word in Tiger books. I flew to Los Angeles with Ian, who had driven the Sunbeam Tiger in European rallies extensively, and we got on famously from the off.

From the airport, we went to RMS *Queen Mary* at Long Beach and stayed on board for one night, where we hooked up with Graham Vickery and his wife, Ruth. Graham is a great friend and currently a trustee of the Rootes Heritage Trust.

Three cars were shipped from England: David Duncanson's ex-works rally Tiger, a Tiger that ran in the 1964 Le Mans 24 Hours race and Graham Vickery's production Tiger, the last one built.

Norman Miller lent us his own Tiger. I asked before we left if we had enough petrol to get us to the first stop and he replied that the petrol gauge read low and assured me we had enough. We hadn't got far when I tapped the gauge to find it firmly stuck at zero and I knew we were in trouble. We were in the middle of an eight-lane highway, with huge trucks on either side of us. The little Tiger only came up to the top of the wheels of the trucks and it was quite scary to be down there, looking up. I managed to negotiate my way across the lanes and in front of us was a filling station up a steep incline. We stopped dead at the foot of the slope and the attendants came down and pushed the Tiger up to the pumps. Though it was nerve-wracking at the time, Norman and I had a laugh about it afterwards.

From then on everything was plain sailing and we arrived in Eureka, North California, three days later, after driving 700 miles upstate. I drove most of the time as Ian was a little erratic on the highways!

The Eureka Inn was our home for the next three days. Originally built in 1922, it had been splendidly renovated over the years, all black beams and white walls. There were no curtains on the windows, just slatted wooden blinds, which I do not like, but apart from that the accommodation was very good.

We had a great time in Eureka and the food and hospitality were wonderful. There were all sorts of fun events over the next few days, with everyone admiring all the beautiful Tigers. People addressed them as if they were old trusted friends. The love and care that went into maintaining those beautiful cars was truly amazing. I gave a talk one evening, recounting stories of the early years rallying all over the world, and it went down very well. Next day I impressed everybody with my performance in the Le Mans Sunbeam Tiger at a local race track, and by the end to my amazement I had acquired a few fans. Next day I gave drives to anybody willing to pay for the privilege and all the money went to a local charity.

It was attending the Tigers United event in 1997, in Eureka, that led to the invitation by SUNI (Sunbeams United National International). Before this, I believe the Americans didn't appreciate or understand European rallying and knew little about my achievements. I am very proud to say I am currently the honorary president of the UK Sunbeam Tiger Owners Club.

At the request of SUNI, I returned to the United States many times. SUNI meetings are aimed at the US community of Sunbeam enthusiasts (Sunbeam being the marque range of the Rootes Group with the most sales in the US). Every five years, from July 1989, a group of enthusiastic Sunbeam owners and drivers have gathered together in various parts of America, from Colorado to South Dakota, for the SUNI. I was invited to attend on many occasions but there are two meetings I remember most vividly, one in Colorado Springs in 2014 to celebrate 50 years of the Tiger and the other in Park City, Utah, in 2004.

The SUNI IV in Park City, in 2004, was where I met the legendary Carroll Shelby, a car designer, racing driver and entrepreneur. Shelby had put a Ford V8 engine into the Sunbeam Alpine car in the early 1960s and he was there with the mechanic, George Boskoff, who did all the technical work to make it happen. They sat side by side on the podium and gave their version of events. George had flown in from Hawaii for the occasion.

The story of how a Ford engine was put into a British-made chassis is a remarkable one. Rootes' USA west coast manager, Ian Garrad, the son of Norman Garrad, who was competition manager for Rootes, talked with Shelby, who said that he could fit a Ford V8 engine into the Sunbeam Alpine, having done similar miracles with the Cobra. This is where Boskoff came into his own when he explained that the firewall had to be modified to create additional space, along with new rack-and-pinion steering and more. These modifications allowed Shelby to fit a 260 cubic inch (4.3l), 164 horsepower V8 into the Sunbeam Alpine body, the result being the Sunbeam Tiger.

Brian Rootes, the son of Lord Rootes, knew what Ian Garrad was planning, but this had all been going on without the approval of his father. Ian had the Shelby prototype shipped over from America in July 1963. The Rootes team were testing the car, but Lord Rootes insisted on driving the car himself. It took only four hours, Shelby said, for Lord Rootes to decide to go ahead and he telephoned Henry Ford directly to place an order for 3,000 V8 Ford engines. That was the number of cars he estimated he could sell in a year. Jensen in West Bromwich in the UK was given the job of manufacturing the Sunbeam and produced 7,085 of them, from 1964 to 1967. That's where it ended because less than six months after the Tiger was introduced, Chrysler, who had by this time taken over Rootes, dropped the car because they couldn't bear to have a Ford engine in a car manufactured under Chrysler management (or so the story goes).

Shelby was guest of honour at the banquet at the end of the week and he turned up in dungarees and a check shirt, with a straw sticking out of his mouth. Well, I suppose that's understandable as he started his career as a chicken farmer, and in any case the Americans didn't seem to dress for dinner in Colorado. Shelby was signing autographs and charged $5 for the privilege, all the proceeds going to his charity, the Carroll Shelby Foundation, which financed organ transplants for children.

There were some interesting sightseeing and cultural events organised and one of them was a visit to a Mormon church in Park City. The acoustics were amazing, and as we sat and listened to the choir I was transported. I got chatting to an American woman, who told me that she had been to Dublin to look for two of their young missionaries, who had gone missing some years before. I remembered then that my mother used to feed two young Mormon men in her home in Dundrum. They had called at the door and she told them that she didn't believe in their religion, but took pity on them and asked them in. Every Thursday evening they came for dinner for months until one day they said they were moving on to the north of Ireland and she never heard from them again. Soon after, my mother died and I couldn't believe it when they arrived at her funeral. I told the American lady that I was convinced those two young men were the ones she had been looking for, and never found.

Graham Robson, the author of numerous motoring books, and I were guests on a trip to the SUNI VI in Colorado, in 2014, and were asked to give a talk one evening during the week-long event. One of the reasons this trip stays in my mind was because it included a drive up Pikes Peak in the Colorado Mountains. Graham and I were driven in an air-conditioned modern car by the man who lent us the Tiger to the top of the Peak, where the altitude left us breathless. We were advised not to jump out of the car immediately but to wait a while until we became acclimatised.

It is a 19-mile highway, which takes you up to a height of 4,302m (14,110 feet) at the summit, with 156 danger-ous corners on the way. The road was gravel and only partly paved at the time although it is now fully paved, I believe. The scenery is breathtaking and inspired Katherine Lee Bates in 1893 to write that very famous American song

'America the Beautiful', otherwise known as Pikes Peak. There is a plaque in the visitors' centre at the summit with the words of the song commemorating her visit there. The visitors' centre was very interesting, with all sorts of memorabilia displayed. It was a wonderful experience, and before we left we were all given passports to say we had gone into space!

All the cars had to complete the ascent before we were allowed to go down again. The temperature at the top of the mountain was −5° Celsius, and halfway down it was hot enough to affect the brakes! Officials stopped all the cars at the halfway point to test the brakes. Our car was too hot and we stayed there for 20 minutes to cool down. The strange thing was we were in a modern car, but the Tigers were fine and the temperature didn't affect their brakes.

In 2014 the Sunbeam Tiger Owners Club (STOC) organised a number of events throughout the year to celebrate the 50th anniversary of the launch of the Sunbeam Tiger. As honorary president of STOC, I was asked to lead a touring rally from England to Monte Carlo. More than 30 Tigers set off from Calais and Pauline Gullick and I drove in an ex-works rally car, which, although well prepared, broke down 100 miles into France. Graham Vickery and his wife Ruth gave us their Tiger, while they stayed behind and tried to get the other car going. When I found that Graham's car was left-hand drive and had been specially upgraded with power steering, which is unusual, I was delighted. I knew this would take the hard work out of the rest of the journey, or so I thought.

Coming behind us were Bill Rogers and Peter Valentine. Bill had come over from America for the event in his Tiger. We were up in the Alps when our throttle cable snapped, and that looked like the end for us. Bill and Peter pulled up and by some miracle they had a spare left-hand-drive throttle cable, which they set about installing. I stood on the sidelines doing nothing but urging them to hurry up. Eventually we were on our way again, and considering the mishaps I was happy when we came in third overall. It was a wonderful event and I enjoyed every minute of it. I adore the Tiger and some day I hope to own one.

The following year, in May 2015, in recognition of my win, 50 years ago, I was honoured to be invited by the organisers of the famous International Historic Tulpenrallye to take part, but unfortunately my former success was not to be repeated. The course had been extended since the time I won it, 50 years earlier, and now started in Italy and ended six days later, in Holland.

When I accepted, I thought I would be driving a Sunbeam Tiger with power steering. I had broken my collarbone a few months earlier, having tripped over some bedclothes in a hotel; no, I was not drunk! The doctors at the hospital put my arm in a sling, which I avoided using as much as possible, of course. The collarbone wasn't completely healed by the time the Tulip came along and the car provided for me was an MGB, which I stupidly assumed would have power steering like the Sunbeam Tiger, but it hadn't. Peter Rushforth, an old friend and rally driver, was a darling and had provided his beautiful 1965 MGB, liveried in British Racing Green, which signified the Irish connection, together with a man to be my co-driver, who, unfortunately, was not so charming.

I flew to Geneva to meet up with the car and my co-driver, who had driven the car from England. When I got into that MGB and started to drive out of the airport, every time I tried to change gear the car stopped. The man beside me was quite cross and asked in a most unpleasant voice, 'Don't you know how to drive these cars? Put it into gear first and then turn the engine on.' But I knew something was very wrong with the car, it wasn't just me, and I was right. When the mechanics had a look at it, they drained the oil in the clutch and refilled it. Apparently the MGB had been lying idle for 18 months and that hadn't helped.

My co-driver kept telling me how wonderful he was as a driver and navigator and saying, of course, 'Things were different in your day.' Of course they were, you have better and faster cars now and more safety regulations in place, I thought. His patronising tone was so annoying and when, after a particularly gruelling stage where there must have been about 100 hairpins, he said, 'You did that quite well,' I could have killed him. The whole drive was turning into a chapter of accidents – not real accidents, but things just kept going from bad to worse – and my co-driver was a handicap. I got to the stage where I could hardly move my left arm, and that was the one I was using to change gear. Trying to haul the car around the hairpin bends was taking its toll on me.

After a long drive in the mountains, we came to a stop for lunch. I was red in the face and could hardly lift my fork. The TV crews were following us around and looking for an interview, but I couldn't face it. I just put up my hand and refused to talk to any of them, which wasn't like me at all. I told Peter I couldn't go on as I was afraid I might put the car off the road and I didn't want to take a chance. I think my co-driver was not sorry to hear this as the next thing I heard he had gone off to Germany, but he said he would be back for the finish.

I was out of the running, but I struggled on through a lot of rain, with the help of some lovely women marshals, who, when we came to a toll road, would get out and put the money in to save me having to get out of the car as all the booths were on the left and my car was a right-hand drive. When we eventually arrived at the hotel in Noordwijk, my co-driver hadn't returned from Germany, as he said he would. All I wanted was to go over the ramp and receive my bunch of tulips! I borrowed a lovely young man to sit beside me in the car; into the finish we went and the tulips were duly handed over.

When I got back to Ireland, I went straight to the Beacon Hospital. The orthopaedic surgeon informed me that my collarbone had come asunder and he would have to put a plate in place to assist the healing process. I really enjoyed those few days in the hospital being fussed over – I needed them after the ordeal of driving through Holland with a collarbone in pieces and an unsympathetic companion. If I had had a good car, two good arms and a pleasant co-driver, I would have absolutely adored it.

In Easter 2016 a Circuit Déjà Vu was organised to commemorate the glory days of the Circuit of Ireland in the 1960s. It was a fun, one-day event, beginning and ending in Killarney, and covering some of the special stages of the Circuit. My co-driver was Mark Dixon, who I had last driven with 22 years before in a Classic Marathon to Czechoslovakia. He was charming and told me I hadn't changed a bit! It was great to meet up with him, Jimmy McRae, Russell Brookes, Adrian Boyd, Paddy Hopkirk and many more of the drivers from the old days. We talked about our experiences in the 1960s and 1970s, shared a few drinks and a lot of laughs.

I loved all those classic rallies and I am very lucky to have been asked to participate in so many of them. The last 15 years have been full of fun and laughter, during which I have experienced some of the best times in my whole life. I have mellowed, and many people who know me well are happy about that! I am not competing against anyone any more and there is no need to prove myself. There is sadness too, when I think of Mary Foley and her husband, former leading Irish motoring journalist Brian Foley, old friends who are gone, but that's life. The only close family I have left are my cousins, Jill, Celia, Hilary and Noelle. There are always there for me and we meet from time to time to reminisce. My wonderful cousin, Jill, has been a great support to me over the years.

I am so grateful to my friends, who look out for me through sickness and bad weather, and are always there when I need them. The friends I have are genuine and generous and I love them all. Larry Mooney, who I have known for many years, organised a surprise 80th birthday party for me, and I know all those old and new friends would have been there to celebrate with me, but it wasn't to be. I was in hospital, getting another stent inserted, and I have to thank my good friend Janet Taylor and my neighbour Deborah Harpur for their help with that. I missed out on my birthday, but that doesn't matter – I am able to catch up with everyone and we spend time together, setting the world to rights. I happily accept all the kind invitations in Ireland, the UK and around the world. Life is good and I am having a ball.

I have done my best to recall the many highlights and challenges I have encountered over the years and I really thought that nothing more of interest would occur. I have been given four lifetime achievement awards and I continue to give talks to interested motoring organisations, drive in classic car rallies, accept the odd accolade and make guest appearances at motor shows and dinners. Nothing out of the ordinary, until 2017, the year of my 80th birthday, when things took off again.

CHAPTER 21

PASSION FOR LIFE

IN 2017 IT was a great honour to be included in the photographic exhibitions and books of two very talented women. The first was on International Women's Day in March, when in Dublin Castle Beta Bajgart showed her series of beautiful portraits of strong and inspirational women at work. There was a firefighter, a pilot, a chess player and many more, including myself, posing beside a car dressed in full motoring gear. The book, *A Woman's Work*, is a beautifully presented coffee table book, which I cherish.

The other exhibition, 'Portrait of a Century', was held in the National Museum of Ireland, Collins Barracks, and was opened by the President, Michael D. Higgins. Kim Haughton was the photographer who had the brilliant idea of seeking out people with a connection to Ireland. Each photograph represents the birth year of the person portrayed and spans 100 years, from 1916 to 2015. I was honoured to be asked to represent 1937, the year of my birth. A magnificent book of the photographs was produced, which not only includes many famous people, but also children and others not in the public eye. I was so flattered to be included in both of these books and sat back, very pleased with myself, thinking, if nothing else occurs this year, I am happy. But my life doesn't seem to work like that and a chance meeting was to set me off on an exciting and unexpected adventure.

It's funny how things happen. When I was introduced to James Boyer, a gorgeous Frenchman, I never would have thought that the brief conversation we had would put me in the public eye again. At the age of 79, I was to become the oldest person ever to drive in a Formula 1 car.

I met James, marketing director with Renault, at a dinner in the Powerscourt Hotel in Enniskerry, at the 2017 Irish Car of the Year Awards. We chatted about this and that, my experiences of my rallying days, and he must have been impressed because a few weeks later I got a call from Paddy McGee, country operations manager for Renault Ireland, who said he had been speaking with James. They had decided between them that it would be amazing if they could make a documentary of me driving a Formula 1 car to celebrate Renault's 40th anniversary. 'Would you be up for it?' he asked.

It was 40 years ago that Renault introduced the first Formula 1 turbo engine at the 1977 Silverstone Grand Prix and truly an occasion for celebration. I laughed at Paddy's suggestion and said, 'That really is a fantastic idea. It would be a miracle if you could make that happen. But you know me, if you can organise it, I'm up for anything.' I never thought for one moment that he was serious.

The French Grand Prix in 2018 was held at the Circuit Paul Ricard at Le Castellet, near Marseille, where Renault Sports' base is situated. Renault had formed a partnership with Winfield Racing School, which was offering motorsport fans a chance to take instruction and drive racing cars, but I never once thought I might be one of them. They were offering to give me, a 79-year-old woman, ex-rally driver, ex-most things at this stage of my life, the chance to drive a Formula 1 car and be the star in a documentary. How could I refuse?

Colin Hickson, head of Light Entertainment with Publicis Worldwide in London, the oldest and one of the largest marketing and communications companies in the world, was chosen to organise and implement the making of the documentary. Colin is a charming man, and when he telephoned to ask if I would like to bring someone with me I immediately thought of my friend June Miller. She is the ideal companion, the perfect person to travel with – we both like a glass of wine and share the same sense of humour. All the travel and hotel arrangements came by email and everything was organised seamlessly. Someone telephoned to ask for my measurements for the driving suit. I have one, I told them, but it had Ford written all over it, so that wouldn't do. I think it was then that it hit me that this was for real: I was going to be fitted for a new driving suit, I was going to drive a Formula 1 car and I was going to be filmed doing it. What had I let myself in for?

June lives in County Meath, which is close to the airport, so I went to stay with her on the night before we left for France. She was excited and really looking forward to a few days in France and the adventure ahead of us. I wasn't so sure. Some of my other friends wouldn't have enjoyed it because it was too much like hard work – for a start, we had to get up at 2.30 a.m. to go to the airport. As usual, my bracelet went clang, clang as we went through Security. Thank heavens that machine couldn't pick up the noise of my heart thumping in my chest at the thought of what I had agreed to. Was I mad? Yes, I suppose the answer has to be yes, but I could never resist a challenge and getting older hasn't changed that.

When we arrived in Marseille we were collected by a driver and taken to the hotel, about an hour's journey away. The Hotel du Castellet is truly magnificent. We met up with some of the people involved in the making of the documentary and had lunch in the luxurious surroundings of the hotel until the car came to take us to the Circuit Paul Ricard. So far, so good! When I stepped out of the car, I could see the faces of the young mechanics and I imagine they were thinking, is this oul wan really going to drive one of our Formula 1 cars, or is someone having a laugh? I certainly wasn't laughing because by this stage I was getting nervous. But there was no way I was going to chicken out.

I'm here now, I said to myself. I'm going to do it, even if it kills me.

When we arrived at the circuit, the first person I saw was Alain Prost, the famous Formula 1 champion. I had met him before years ago and I thought, there is no way he is going to remember me. But I was wrong; at least I think I was. He came towards me, 'Oh Rosemaree, I haven't seen you for so long,' he said in his lovely French accent. I don't know if he really remembered me or if people had told him who I was, but in any case it was wonderful to be made a fuss of by such a great man. When we had our photograph taken together I had to bend down as I towered over him. Alain is about 5'4" and only came up to my shoulder. He is exactly the right size for a Formula 1 driver; there is not much room to spare inside those cars!

As I looked around, I was really chuffed when I saw the initials RS all over the place: on the cars, on the side of the trucks, on my driving suit, everywhere. I said to Colin Hickson, 'How wonderful that they have gone to the trouble of putting my initials on everything!' He laughed and said, 'Sorry, Rosie, that stands for Renault Sports.' Silly me, the ego was out of control!

I didn't drive at all that day, but instead was shown around the marvellous grandstand, which seats 4,000 spectators, and introduced to the mechanics and the rest of the crew, who were making the documentary. They fitted me for a seat belt, which comprised a six-point harness, which can be released with a single hand movement, in case you need to get out of the car in a hurry. There were forms to be filled in and I noticed the one which said that the maximum age for a driver of a Formula 1 car was 65. I pointed to that and Colin assured me it was OK, they had cleared it with the circuit officials.

Everything was so well organised and everyone was so kind and welcoming that I thought my anxiety levels might improve, but when we went back to the hotel that night to have dinner I just took three mouthfuls of soup and had to excuse myself and go up to the bedroom. I couldn't eat. It had been a long day and, while I couldn't stomach any food, I also needed to rest if I was going to do justice to the mission I had undertaken. Thankfully, I fell into bed and went straight to sleep. The car came to take us to the circuit early next morning and I was up and ready for action. We had breakfast of coffee and croissants as the drones and helicopter flew overhead, movie cameras following my every move. I was the centre of attraction and I must say I loved that. When you get to my age, it doesn't happen too often!

Charlie, the track manager, a really lovely woman, brought me down to get dressed. The Winfield driver suits were on one side and the Renault ones on the other. Boxes and boxes of helmets, suits, underwear, gloves in every size were stacked up. Anyone coming to the track to practise would be well kitted out. First, I put on the fireproof underwear, then the suit, which was black with yellow stripes with a high neck – it made me look quite slim, which was great. The red boots were next and then the balaclava, gloves, and finally the helmet was selected. There were lots of takes and retakes and the film crew seemed to especially like my pulling on the gloves and flashing my long red nails. Someone said I should be careful they didn't come loose and fall off. I had to explain that they were all mine and I never went near a manicurist, but looked after them myself. The eyelashes had been attached, I told them, but not the nails. All the time I was dressing and being filmed, I just hoped they didn't see my heart jumping out of my suit, and once again I was thinking, why had I agreed to this?

All suited and booted, I was ready to be introduced to my instructor, Tom Crooke, who was an absolute darling. He was a very patient and considerate man and I was happy to take instruction from him – I needed every bit of help I could get. I climbed into the Clio RS, a lovely little car, and sat beside him as we drove around the track and he showed me the bends. Tom had walked the track the night before and put cones on the apex of the various corners. 'When you see two red ones, brake immediately,' he told me. We did about four laps and he said, 'Can you remember all that?' I replied, 'You say nothing and I'll call the bends as we come up to them,' which I did: 'Sharp right, hairpin left,' and so on. Remembering the turns was no problem to me. It was just like in the rallying days when we would do a recce and have to remember where all the twists and turns would occur when we did it for real.

That was the easy part over and everything was going well. The next stage was to drive in the Formula Renault single-seater, which has about one fifth of the power of the Formula 1 car, but looked pretty much the same. Getting into the car was an ordeal in itself; lifting my legs and stepping over those side pods was the first handicap. It was the most inelegant thing ever and I hoped they would cut that bit out of the film. Once I was in the car, I had to sit and slide myself further and further down. As I slid down into position, all I could see was the little steering wheel shaped like a bow and the instructor explained to me that the gears were behind the wheel, up this way and down the other. I had to take all this in before I even started to physically drive the car.

Another very senior track official, Yves, drove in front of me in the Clio to ascertain how well I was able to navigate the bends and pronounced me competent, which was a compliment coming from such a high-ranking executive. I believe that if he had not given his approval the whole thing would have been a non-runner.

I did about six laps and it was decided that I was perfectly capable of getting behind the wheel of the actual Formula 1 car. There was a briefing room upstairs and a video which showed me everything all over again. Everyone did all they could to make sure I was ready for the experience and I really appreciated that – I wasn't exactly afraid, I just wanted to get on with it. I was about to put my leg into the car when my good friend Pauline Gullick came around the corner and into the pit lane. The organisers had kindly brought her over, and when she saw me she burst into tears. Not sure why. Maybe she thought this was the last time she would see me alive!

The organisers were hoping that the Guinness World Records would have been there, but they had left it too late to get them, so it didn't happen. What would the entry have been: the oldest person to drive a Formula 1 car and survive? Jolyon Palmer, who is a gorgeous young man, very tall and charming just like his father, Jonathan, a Formula 1 driver, who I knew in the old days, suggested he would carry me on a special attachment they can put at the back of another Formula car. That was the only thing I said no to; I was going to do it on my own and if I made a mistake there was nobody to blame but myself. At the back of my mind I was thinking about the cost of building a Formula 1 car and the expense involved if I did it damage.

The whole process of getting into the car began again and those mechanics and everyone else were so kind as they helped the old lady into the driving seat once again and I wiggled my way down into the car. A brace was put around my neck and the helmet was pulled very tight. My legs are so long and to say it was a snug fit would be an understatement! There was little leg room and even less arm room, but with the small steering wheel that didn't matter too much. 'Push down further,' one of the mechanics said. 'If I go any further, my feet would be coming out of the nose of the car,' I replied. They adjusted the seat belt and it was so tight that it felt as if the car and I were welded together; snug as a bug in the proverbial rug.

The mechanics wheeled me out of the garage into the pit lane. My helmet was adjusted and plugs put in my ears because the noise those cars make is unbelievable. I also had this contraption in my ear so that the instructor could talk to me as I went around. You have to kind of imagine where the front wing is as you are so low down in the car, your vision is impeded. The mechanic put his finger on the wheel and asked could I see it? 'I can, just about,' I replied, and that was good enough.

Pauline needn't have worried; there was a safety car on every corner, and if there was an accident, I was assured that they could be with me in 40 seconds. As well as that there was an ambulance and doctors at the ready. Just before I went out, a senior mechanic, Josh, leaned in the car, pointed down and said, 'Have they told you about this little red button?' I shook my head. 'Don't touch it,' he said as I put my hand towards it. 'If the car bursts into flames, just pull it.' That really helped my nerves. Apparently, it activates a suppression system, which spreads fire retardant foam around the chassis and engine.

I had been told by everyone that a lot of first-time drivers, including Jeremy Clarkson, stall the car and even those who have driven it before do it too. I was determined not to make that mistake and I think that's what impressed the mechanics, who had witnessed so many amateurs struggling. Tom was talking into my earphones as I started out.

I could hear his voice in my ear: 'You're in first gear, let the clutch out gently, gently.' I did that and then I misheard his next instruction. He was saying, 'Press down on the accelerator,' and I was coming off it. I quickly got that right as he yelled again, 'Down, down,' and away we went.

I was off! It was exhilarating and the nervousness left me once I got going. A little camera was attached to the left-hand side of the car, which is fine when you are looking straight ahead, but when I went into a tight left-hand bend it blocked the track from sight. It was a slight handicap, but the least of my worries. I loved every minute of it and I am not saying it was easy but all my experience over the years stood to me. I had to concentrate on the driving and listen to the instructions coming into my ear, which is not easy: the car is going so fast and your brain just has to keep up.

After about 15 laps the red flag was waved for me to stop. I turned the engine off and the car drifted in. It was over!

What a wonderful experience, and I would do it again if I had the chance. I know now that driving a Formula 1 car is not a big evil thing that will gobble me up. It is such a safe circuit and I felt secure and trusted the pit crew and everyone involved. When I was in the car, I wasn't frightened. It is second nature to me and I could see the people in the pit lane on the periphery of my vision, and the one thing I kept thinking was, don't make a fool of yourself. Of course, everyone asks what speed I went; I know it wasn't that fast, but I wasn't looking at the speedometer to find out.

When I got back to the pit, as two lovely young men were helping me out of the car, I said, 'Get me out of this goddam coffin!' I'm sure they will cut that out of the film; at least I hope so. As I stood up, my knees were knocking and I was so happy to see before me a semi-circle of around 50 people, all clapping, hugging and cheering me. It was a very special feeling; I think they must have thought I would never do it and they appreciated the enormity of what I had achieved. I felt so happy that I had not disgraced myself. I think I could get used to driving a Formula 1 car very easily and maybe go even faster next time.

We had lunch upstairs in the gorgeous restaurant, where there were photographs of past and present drivers on the wall. Still in my suit, I was smiling all the time, like a cat that had got the cream. We did some more filming and Pauline was interviewed. The two of us sat in the corporate box like motor racing royalty. When we got back to the hotel I needed a drink, and so I had a glass of wine and then another and went upstairs for a rest before dinner, but the adrenaline was still coursing through my body and I couldn't relax.

To finish the day, the whole team climbed into cars and went down to a restaurant in Bandol for dinner. As I sat, surrounded by all the people who had made this happen, it came to me what a momentous event it really was and I was just delighted that I was able to do it for Renault. I got a text from James Boyer of Renault, who had set the whole thing in motion, saying, 'You seem to be having great fun.' I replied, 'Thanks, still alive, but heart-stopping.'

ACKNOWLEDGEMENTS

Rosemary

My sincere thanks to all my wonderful friends, all the motoring people and everybody I've met along the way, who have encouraged me to tell my story. I am indebted to the RIAC, especially Alex Sinclair and Arthur Collier (Chairman), not forgetting, of course, the lovely staff in the restaurant and garage for their kindness. I would like to thank my old friend Eddie Jordan for his generous fore-word. I am grateful to Renault Ireland for its support and for giving me the amazing opportunity to represent them and make history in the Formula 1 drive. My thanks too to the Jameson Distillery at Bow Street. I wouldn't be here at all if it wasn't for the wonderful staff of the Beacon, St Vincent's Hospital and the Blackrock Clinic. They kept me alive, and Ann and Judy of Peter Marks Hairdressers in Dundrum kept me looking good.

Finally, I would like to thank Ann Ingle most sincerely for putting up with me for a year and a half while she was writing my story. She's the kindest, most generous person – and very patient. Without her this book would never have been written. My 'Mrs Ghost'.

Ann

Thanks to Paul Howard for introducing me to Rosemary and for his unequivocal belief that I was the woman for the job. I am grateful to my early readers, June Finegan and the members of the PS Writers Group, for their encouragement. The insights of Sarah Ingle and Willo Roe were invaluable. Thanks to Faith O'Grady, of the Lisa Richards Agency, for recognising that Rosemary had a great story to tell and to Eoin McHugh, of HarperCollins, for making it happen. Meeting Rosemary Smith and working with her has been a privilege and an unforgettable experience. Thanks, Rosemary, for all the laughs along the way.

ABOUT THE AUTHORS

Rosemary Smith

Rosemary Smith is a rally driver from Dublin. Her father taught her to drive at the age of 11 in a field in Tallaght. Leaving school at 15, Rosemary trained as a dress designer and model and opened a boutique dressmaking company. Rosemary was asked to navigate for a friend in a rally but soon took over the driving due to her inability to read a map. She went on to drive in the Monte Carlo rally eight times, winning the Coupe des Dames on numerous occasions as well as competing in other iconic events all over the world, including the London to Sydney Marathon Rally in 1968, the World Cup London to Mexico Rally in 1970 and the East African Safari Rally in the 1970s. In a Hillman Imp, Rosemary won the Tulip Rally outright, beating all the male drivers to the finish.

Rosemary is passionate about road safety and in 1999 opened the Rosemary Smith School of Motoring, where she teaches young people to drive. In 2017, at 80 years of age, she became the oldest person to drive a Renault Sports Formula 1 team car.

Ann Ingle

Ann was born in London in 1939 and came to live in Ireland after marrying Peter, who died in 1980. After raising her family of eight, Ann completed a BA(Hons) in English and History at Trinity College Dublin. She has been writing and editing ever since. Ann is currently working on her memoir.

INDEX

Page references in *italics* indicate images.
RS indicates Rosemary Smith.

Aaltonen, Rauno 6, 70
Acropolis Rally (1965) 64–5, 70
Adams, Ronnie 38
Aintree Motor Racing Circuit 3, 174
Aitken, Sir Max 111
Altamont, Jeremy Ulick Brown, 11th Marquess of Sligo 174–5
Amies, Hardy 27
Andretti, Mario 92
An Post 217
Ardmore Studios 53
Austin-Healey 67, 91
 'Frogeye' Sprite 91
 3000 73–4, 229
Austin Maxi 129, 130, 131–2, 133, 137, 143, 144, 213
Australian Sydney Telegraph 112
Automobile Club de l'Ouest 62–3
Automobile Club of Peru 139

Bajgart, Beta 243; *A Woman's Work* 243
Balfe, Terry 152
Bates, Katherine Lee 235–6
BBC 97, 99, 123
Beatles 32
Belgium Grand Prix (1998) 217

Bettystown, Ireland 16
Bigger, Delphine 38–9, 41–5, 46–7, 50, 51, 52, 54
Bigger, Frank 38, 45–6, 47
Birrell, Jennifer 92
Blaney, Neil 132
Blomqvist, Stig 3
BMW 91
Bord Fáilte 174–6
Borgnine, Ernest 86
Boskoff, George 233
Bousquet, Annie 62
Boyd, Adrian 50, 240
Boyer, James 6, 244, 255
Brands Hatch Circuit 96–7, 183
Brennan, Séamus 197–8
British Institute of Dress Designing 27
British Leyland 129–30, 132, 133, 134, 136
British Motor Corporation (BMC) 66, 70, 118, 134–5, 143
British Wool Marketing Board 113
Brookes, Russell 240
Brown, David 105
Burton, Richard 73, 76
Byrne, Kate 53, 54

Cabot, David 174, 175
CanTeen 228–9
Carrigrohane Straight 177, 178
Carroll Shelby Foundation 234
Casey, Bishop 203

Catholic Church 205, 221
CBS 84
Chevron B16 92
Chrysler Corporation 79, 81, 84, 85, 86, 105, 107, 108, 234
Circuit Déjà Vu 240
Circuit of Ireland Rally 47–50, 51, 65, 69, 112, 240
Circuit of Leinster 43
Circuit Paul Ricard 6, 245, 246
Clark, Jim 2, 3
Clarke, Roger 3, 49–50, 166
Clarkson, Jeremy 252
Classic Car 50
classic/historic rallies 225–41
Clotworthy, Pauline 27–8
Connolly, Sybil 28
Coombe, Anne 88, 89
Cooper, Sally Anne 55, 56, 57, 58–9, 62
Cornwell, Mike 229
Coupe des Alpes (Alpine Rally) 70, 76–8
Coupe des Dames 69–70, 71, 72, 88, 90, 107, 124, 259
Crean, Peter 201–2
Crooke, Tom 249
Cullen, Bill 180
Cusack, Paul 180
Cutex 35

Dáil Éireann 197
Daily Express 111–12, 130, 150
Daily Mirror 130, 131

Daily Mirror World Cup Rally (1970) 127, 129–44, *131*, *143*
Dalamount, Dean 131
Dalí, Salvador 175
Datsun 1600SSS 164
Dawson, Clark 50
Daytona 24-hour (1966) 81–4
Denton, Jena 139, 143, 144
Desai, Sidia 164, 166, 171
Dickson, Wylton 130
Dietrich, Suzy 82
Dior, Christian 20, 30–1
Dixon, Mark 240
Domleo, Valerie 51, 70, 72, 74, 75, *75*, 99
Donegal Rally 99, 101, 177
Doyle, Pat v, 8, 198, 207
Drolet, Smokey 82, 83
Dublin Castle 243
Duncanson, David 230, 231
Dún Laoghaire-Rathdown County Council 185–6, 187

East African Safari Rally 259
(1973) 163
(1974) 161, 163–72
Eureka Inn, California 231–2

Fairyhouse Racecourse 198
Faith, Adam 8, 32, 33, 34–5
Fall, Tony 137, 142
Federation Internationale de l'Automobile (FIA) 70
Ferrari 91, 92, 215
Foley, Brian 240
Foley, Mary 240
Ford 14, 102, 109, 111, 112, 113, 120, 121, 126, 132, 200, 233, 234, 245
Cortina 74, 117
Cortina Lotus 111, 117, 120, 121, 123, 124, 126
Escort 3, 50, 137, 173, 216
Ford, Henry 234
Forestry Commission 51
Formula Atlantic Championship 173
Formula 1 3, 5–6, 177, 243–55
Fountain, Bruce 230
French Grand Prix (2018) 245
Freud, Clement 217–19

Garrad, Ian 233
Garrad, Norman 59–60, 61, 62, 63, 64–5, 107–8, 233

Garrett, Richard: *Rally-Go-Round, The* 62
Geneva Rally 65
(1964) 72
(1968) 108–9
Gilbert, Irene 28, 29
Goffs 157, 199
Goodwood 96
Grace of Monaco, Princess 28, 59, 69
Grafton Academy of Fashion Design 26–7
Greaves, Jimmy 131, 137, 142
Grosvenor House 155–6
Gubay, Albert 204–5, 206, 207–8, 209
Guinness World Records 251
Gullick, Pauline 99, 100, 101, 161, 163, 165, 166–7, 168, 169, 170, 195–6, 216, 229, 236, 250–1, 252, 254
Guthrie, Janet 82, 91, 92

Halda 102
Hall, Anne 78, 229
Hall, Ian 230, 231
Hanstein, Fritz Huschke von 108
Hardy, Joe 126
Harley, Keane 199
Harper, Peter 73
Harpur, Deborah 241
Harrison, Captain David 117
Hartnell, Norman 27
Haughey, Charles 132, 154
Haughey, Maureen 154
Haughton, Kim 243
Heath, Edward 132–3
Hefner, Hugh 218
Hickson, Colin 245, 247, 248
Higgins, Michael D. 243
Highgate Private Hospital, London 191
Hill, Damon 217
Hill, Graham 3, 156
Hill, Mick 177
Hillman Imp 3, 49, *49*, 50, 65–6, 69, 73, 76, 87–8, 95, 98–9, 107, 217, 226
Historic Motorsports Show, Stoneleigh Park 202
Hope, Bob 86, 87
Hopkirk, Paddy 2, 6, 64, 69, 70–1, 123, 130, 134, 180, 217, 240
Hotel du Castellet, France 246

Ice race, Sweden, televised 97–101
Imp Club of Ireland 50
International Financial Services Centre (Dublin) 7
International Historic Tulpenrallye 237; *see also* Tulip Rally
International Women's Day (2017) 243
Irish Car of the Year Awards (2017) 244
Irish Grand Prix 217
Irish Independent 191–2
Irish National Land Speed Record (1978) 5, 177–9
Irish Times, The 76, 186
Issigonis, Alec 143

Jackson, Eric 74
Jaguar 97, 177, 178, 179
Janson, Peter 105–7
Jensen 234
Johnston, Derek 38
Jordan, Eddie 1–3, 173–4
Jordan Grand Prix 173
Jorgensen, Ib 31
Joyce, Doris 25

Keany, Danny 177, 178–9
Kellett, Iris 24
Kemsley, Jack 124, 126
Kennedy, Jackie 36
Kennedy, John F. 36
Kenneally, Peter 179
Kenny, Anna 187
Kenny, Enda 202–3
Kenny, Tony 180
Kent, HRH Prince Michael of 132, 142
Kingsley, Terry 134
Kondratieff, Judy 91

Le Mans 62–3, 64, 82
(1964) 231, 232
Levegh, Pierre 63
Lewis, Tiny 73
Lombard & Ulster Bank 216
London to Sydney Marathon Rally (1968) 102, 109, 111–27, 129
Lotus
Elan 96–7, 173
Sunbeam 99, 101
Lynch, Jack 132

Mackenzie, Margaret 69, 70, 72, 77–8

Macmillan Ring Free Motor Racing Oil 81–2, 84
Mäkinen, Timo 67, 70
Malone, Joe 175
Mazda 226, 228
McAleese, Mary 220
McClintock, Paddy 179
McCurtain, Marguerite 180
McGee, Paddy 6, 244–5
McIndoe, Sir Archibald 96
McQueen, Steve 91–2
McRae, Jimmy 101, 240
Mercedes SSK 217
Mespil Flats, Dublin 52
Metropole Hotel, Monte Carlo 214
MG
  MGA 229
  MGB 237–8
Mikkola, Hannu 143
Miller, June 245, 246
Miller, Norman 230, 231
Mills, Jonathan 97
Mims, Donna Mae 82
Mini 2, 43, 44, 45, 66, 70, 132
Mini Cooper 50, 51, 66, 217
Miriam Woodbyrne Modelling Agency 30–1
Mitsubishi Classic Marathon 229–30
Molyneux, Brian 216
Monaghan Rally 101–3
Mondello Park 176, 182, 203
Monte Carlo Rally 2, 15, 48, 63, 78, 112, 213
  (1927) 70
  (1951) 66
  (1956) 38
  (1962) 55–60
  (1963) 66–70
  (1964) 69, 217
  (1965) 38, 70
  (1966) 70–2
  (1967) 72
  (1968) 72
  Coupe des Dames 69–70, 71
Mooney, Larry 241
Moore, Bobby 129
Mormon church, Park City 234–5
Moss, Pat 70, 97
Moss, Stirling 59, 70, 229
Motorways 179
MS Verdi 140
Mullard Motor Cycle and Car Club 216

Murphy, Eileen 191, 194, 201
Murphy, Mike 202–3

New Zealand 204, 219, 220
Norwood, John 81, 82

O'Callaghan, Deirdre 176
O'Dell, Des 87, 88, 89
O'Hara, Maureen 86, 86
O'Kelly, Seán T. 29

Palm, Gunnar 143
Palmer, Jonathan 251
Palmer, Jolyon 251
Paul Ricard circuit 3, 6, 245, 246
Phoenix magazine 183–4
Phoenix Park, Dublin 52–3, 176, 217, 221
Pikes Peak, Colorado 235–6
Pointet, Lucette 112–13, 114–15, 116, 117, 119, 121–2, 126
Porsche 911 1, 108–9
'Portrait of a Century' exhibition, National Museum of Ireland, Collins Barracks (2017) 243–4
Procter, Peter 96
Procter, Shirley 96
Prost, Alain 247
Proudlock, Lieutenant Martin 117
Provisional IRA 132
Publicis Worldwide 245

RAC 131
RAC Rally 50–2, 148
  (1961) 50, 51–2, 55
  (1965) 50, 70
  (1966) 2–3, 51
Rainier III of Monaco, Prince 59, 71
Ramsey, Sir Alf 129
Red Arrows 132, 134, 142
Reed, Oliver 53–4
Reeves, Susan 50–1
R. E. Hamilton 216
Renault 180, 200, 244
  Clio 200, 249, 250
  Renault F1 3, 5, 6, 245–55
  Renault Ireland 244
  Renault Sports 245, 247
  RS drives a Formula 1 car 244–55
Reynolds, Debbie 86

Riley, Peter 73
Ring, Adrienne 31
Riverdance 180
RMS Queen Mary 230
Robinson, Mary 220
Robson, Graham 235
Roches Stores 38
Rogers, Bill 237
Rogers, Ginger 85
de Rolland, Ginette 108–9, 130, 131, 133, 136, 138–9, 141
Rootes 57, 59, 60, 61, 63–79, 81, 87, 97, 107–8, 149, 156, 230, 232, 233–4
Rootes, Brian 233
Rootes Group 61, 79, 232
Rootes Heritage Trust 230
Rootes, Lord 57, 65, 233–4
rosemarysmith.ie 199
Rosemary Smith School of Motoring 198–200, 201, 208, 219
Rowe, John 68
Royal Air Force Aerobatic Team 132
Royal Automobile Club of the Netherlands 73
Royal Hibernian Hotel 31
Royal Irish Automobile Club (RIAC) 178, 217
Royal Navy 229
RTÉ TV 179
Rushforth, Peter 238
Ryan, Phyllis 28–9

Safari Rally see East African Safari Rally
Sassoon, Vidal 156
Schumacher, Michael 173
Scott, Peter 101–2
Scottish Rally 65; (1970) 144
Sears, Jack 112
Searsons Bar, Dublin 126
Seers, Rosemary 66–9
self-driving cars 7
Shelby, Carroll 233, 234
Shell 4000
  (1966) 87–8
  (1967) 88–90
Sheppard, Cepta 50
Sheppard, John 50
Sheridan, Monica 175
Silverstone 6
  Grand Prix (1977) 244
Skoda 200

DRIVEN

Smith, Jane (mother) 7, 11,
12, 13, 14, 15, 16, 17,
18–21, 22, 26, 27, 30, 31,
33, 42, 59, 61, 93, 96, 114,
147, 148, 152, 156,
159–60, 191, 203, 221–4,
235
Smith, John Metcalf (father)
11–12, 13, 14–15, 16,
18–19, 20, 21, 22, 24, 25,
26, 31, 35, 37, 42, 46, 55,
56, 58, 61, 75, 108, 114,
119, 152, 156, 191, 197,
221, 222, 223
Smith, Noel (cousin) 1
Smith, Pamela (sister) 12,
14–15, 19, 20, 24, 26, 33,
191, 197
Smith, Roger (brother)
12–13, 14–15, 19, 20, 24,
26, 191, 221, 223
Smith, Rosemary
accidents 95–103
appearance viii, 2, 49, 64,
86, 87, 191
birth and childhood 11–22,
23–6
boutique dressmaking
company 31–2, 35, 37–8,
259
collarbone, breaks 237–9
classic/historic rallies and
225–41
coronary artery disease/
stents 6, 202, 205, 241
cosmetic surgery 191–6
death, contemplates 7–9
divorce 161, 181
dressmaking jobs 28–30
80th birthday 241
education 220
engagements 147–50
family see individual family
member name
Formula 1 Renault car,
drives 3, 5–6, 243–55
'Four Winds' house 160,
181, 185–7, 191, 201,
204–9
Grafton Academy of Fashion
Design 26–8
Hollywood and 86, 86, 87
Irish land speed record
177–9
learns to drive 14–15
marriage 93, 144–5, 147,
150–61, 181, 191
modelling 30–1

miscarriages 157, 160, 191,
224
money problems 182–9,
202–9
photographic exhibitions
and books, included in
243–4
postage stamp depicts 217,
218
promotes Ireland as a tourist
destination 174–7
rallying career, birth of 38–9,
41–54
rallying career see individual
race name
rallying cars see individual
car and brand name
recollections and regrets
211–24
Rosemary Smith School of
Motoring 198–200, 201,
208, 219
school days 12, 23–6
shyness 17, 85
TV shows 179–80
Smurfit, Jeff 13–14
Sopwith, Tommy 112
Sprinzel, John 131
SS Chusan 121–3
SS Derwent 133
Stelvio Pass 229
Stewart, Jackie 6
STOA (Sunbeam Tiger
Owners Association) 230
Stokes, Lord 129, 136–7
Stoneleigh Motor Show 96
Stubbs Gazette 183
Sunbeam Alpine 62, 79, 83,
107, 233
Sunbeam Imp 72
Sunbeam Rapier 55, 57–8,
66, 107
Sunbeam Tiger 72, 73, 107,
229–38
Sunbeam Tiger Owners Club
(STOC) 232, 236
SUNI (Sunbeams United
National International)
232–3
IV (2004) 233–5
VI (2014) 235–6
Super Saloons racing 173, 177

Tapley, Una 29–30
Taylor, Elizabeth 76
Taylor, Eve 34
Taylor, Henry 112
Taylor, Janet 241

Theatre Royal, Dublin 32, 33
The Late Late Show
(television show) 180
Think Awareness Transition
Year Driving Programme
198
Tigers United USA 230–2
T. J. Cullen 29–30
Toivonen, Pauli 71, 108
Tour de France Rally 214–15
Tour of Mull 216; (1972)
216–17
Trautmann, Claudine 139
Triumph TR2 147–8
Troubles, Northern Ireland
132
Trouser Lining Company
(TLC) 37–8
Tulip Rally 79
(1949) 73
(1965) 1, 70, 72–6, 74, 107,
217, 237
Turner, Stuart 118, 121,
134–5
12 Hours of Sebring
(1969) 90–1
(1970) 91–2
(1971) 92

Universal Studios 86, 86

Valentine, Peter 237
Van Damm, Sheila 59
Vard, Cecil 66, 156
Vickery, Graham 230, 231,
236–7
Vickery, Ruth 230, 236

Waller, Rod 74, 119
Watson, Alice 130, 131, 132,
133, 136, 137–8, 139, 140,
141, 142, 144–5, 213
Watson, Andy 145
Western Australia Classic
Rally (1994) 225–9
What's My Line? (television
programme) 84–5
Whelan, Bill 180
Whelan, Mairéad 35–7
Wilson, Harold 133
Winfield Racing School 245,
248
Woman 218
Wright, Pat 58, 59

Yamaha 177, 178

Zafer, Alan 134